# REACHING

## FOR THE

# GOLD

# REACHING
## FOR THE
# GOLD

## HOW TO SUCCESSFULLY PREPARE FOR POLICE AND FIRE CHIEF INTERVIEWS

## P. LAMONT EWELL

Foreword by Steve Alexander,
President of The Steve Alexander Group

authorHOUSE®

*AuthorHouse™*
*1663 Liberty Drive*
*Bloomington, IN 47403*
*www.authorhouse.com*
*Phone: 1-800-839-8640*

*Published by AuthorHouse    08/27/2012*

*ISBN: 978-1-4772-6207-8 (sc)*
*ISBN: 978-1-4772-6205-4 (hc)*
*ISBN: 978-1-4772-6206-1 (e)*

*Library of Congress Control Number: 2012915148*

*To Mary, Jam, Nick, Justin, Mom, Jan and Stan;
Thank you for your unwavering support and
encouragement!*

# TABLE OF CONTENTS

# FOREWORD

This is an unusual forward, more about the author than the book. And there's a reason.

To know what you are about to read is worthwhile is to know the person who wrote it. Yet most will not. So, I hope you'll get some sense of the author, and what he has to offer, by reading this forward. To begin, a little story first.

*He walked from behind the dais when he saw me enter the public hearing room. As he leaned in to whisper to me, creating an intimacy that I knew ushered the significance of what he was about to say, I'll never forget these words: "I gave careful consideration to your position on this issue, and though your approach is well thought-out, reasoned, and worthy of pursuing that approach, I'm going to disagree with you publicly and fight for the view I've shared with you in our conversations. I hope you'll respect that. I just thought you ought to know before we begin the hearing. I figured I owed you that much."*

That was P. Lamont Ewell in one of our first encounters. I knew at that point he was a rare person. As the city manager of one of the nation's largest cities, a person of power, of course, and yet with a humility, conscientiousness and compassion that overrode his need to exercise that power insensitively and blindly. He was and is defined by his ethics. His commitment as a public servant (something we've somehow lost in this era of criticism of anything and everything related to government) defined his work during our time together in San Diego. His honesty, consistency of character, pride in doing good work, support of those around him and his openness to professional growth, learning from others, and being more of who he can be were and are the rare qualities that separate leaders from the also-rans.

With this book, readers will hear and see that special character. They will learn the lessons from a true insider's perspective. Someone who has been there, fought the battles, seen the winners and losers, endured criticism and blame, and yet risen, through character and commitment, above it.

Cherish each morsel. Read and re-read. Look for what works, what pushes you beyond your usual view of things. Find and integrate the lessons and insights that will make you a better public servant, a better provider of service to the citizens you serve and your team. As pointed out in the book, sometimes you'll advance, sometimes you'll make the right decisions, and sometimes you'll fail and learn from those failures to do even better in the future.

No matter what, you'll surely be better at what you do when you understand the lessons offered come from a man of conscience, deeply committed to improving himself and others. Because all is offered in the name of public service and the honor that has been for him and the people he has served.

This forward started out with a brief story. A story that described the author and his style. If it wasn't obvious, the key to that style is the finely honed skill of effective communication. Of course, as a communications specialist, I have a bias. I believe all great work in management, teamwork, leadership and working with various communities and constituencies, whether employees, outside stakeholders, the media or others stems from effective communication. This book underscores that message.

Andy Grove, co-founder and former CEO of Intel said, "How well we communicate is determined not by how well we say things, but by how well we are understood." He underscores the fact that communication is not just a two-way process, where one person speaks and the other listens and, when done well, confirms what they heard. Effective communication goes further. It requires a third step where the speaker confirms the listener got it right. Too often we assume this last part. And as leaders we get it wrong.

"Reaching for the Gold" will be worth gold to the reader if they understand the books underlying message about the importance of verbal and non-verbal communication, and how much it contributes to career and life success. Being listened to, heard, and understood is a gift good leaders give to their audience. David W. Augsburger put it more emphatically, "Being heard is so close to being loved that for the average person, they are almost indistinguishable." If this book helps you be a better communicator, no matter what you do, it will also help those around you—peers, subordinates and superiors, communities, elected officials and others—be better at what they do. That's the mark of true leadership.

I work as a coach, trainer, consultant and facilitator for countless private and public agencies, especially in the area of local and state government. I've served as an appointee of three San Diego mayors and three California governors. I know when I've seen someone special, unique and is destined to rise, not just in the political side of those institutions, but in the policy and leadership side as well. When I first met Lamont, he was leading one of the nation's largest cities as its new city manager, and I saw him tackle some of the most complicated problems in the history of our city and cities in the nation. San Diego was one of the first cities to address the depth and breadth of the pending pension and related economic crisis we know throughout the nation today. It's from this perspective that I commend those who have decided to better their careers, commit to public service with a true servant-leadership heart, and pursue the lessons offered in this book.

Through your journey, in addition to learning the tips, skills and insights offered, I hope you'll learn a bit about my friend Lamont. He made a big impact on me and countless others whose lives he's touched in his public service voyage. You'll do well to absorb some of what's in-between the lines as well as the words on the page. If you are in a stage of your career where you are defining what type of leader you want to be . . . this book is definitely for you.

# DEDICATION

This book is dedicated to retired Fire Chief Monroe Smith. He is the most influential male in my personal life and professional career. Considered by many as one of the most progressive public safety leaders of our time, he played a major role in the transformation of the fire service nationwide. He is best known for seeking new and innovative ways of advancing the fire service and more importantly, the women and men within it. He taught through example the value and importance of creating strong relationships between the community, city hall, police department, and public safety departments throughout the region. Most importantly, he instilled in us the courage to always stand for that which is right, to never cower or bend to any threat, to dream big and always pursue our goals.

# Introduction

Government has entered a new era. It is an era of reset. A reset that when fully implemented will dramatically change the way in which government will function forever more. With the unprecedented decline in the world economy, we have experienced financial anarchy worldwide. In the United States it has impacted virtually every level of government. Historically, the United States has experienced many up and down economic cycles. However, with the exception of the 1929 Great Depression, none of the past cycles have rivaled the impacts being experienced today.

At the local levels of government, it has forced officials to begin addressing a myriad of issues that have been peculating just below the surface for several years. The cost of operating government services has skyrocketed over the years creating a negative impact to service levels we have become accustomed to. These costs have necessitated the downsizing of workforces as one means of addressing the increases of such expenses as employee benefits.

Raising local and state taxes in order to pay for desired levels of service has not been politically palatable. The voters of most communities throughout the nation are tax fatigued. Seeking ways to reduce operational costs, without causing further deterioration of service, has become nearly impossible. This has caused many municipalities across the nation to focus their attention on such expenses as the cost of pension systems. In fact, several major cities have now begun to either drastically reduce pension benefits for current and new hires or have called for the elimination of defined pension benefits and the immediate implementation of contribution pension systems such as a 401 (k). This dramatic change includes public safety officers as well. Equally alarming are the number of cities that are now considering bankruptcy protection in an effort to restructure its debt and reopen negotiated labor contracts.

Given such chaos, the skeptical would argue that only the foolish would be interested in a leadership position today. After all, government's best days are well behind us.

However, aspiring public safety leaders refuse to be deterred by these continuously changing environments. They intuitively understand that despite having to face unprecedented economic times, the arc of history will continue to bend forward. They accept the reality that change, no matter how dramatic, is inevitable. They eagerly and enthusiastically embrace change because they continue to see it for what it truly is—an opportunity in disguise. They rise to these challenges instinctively knowing that it is how we choose to respond and not how we react that will make all the difference to potential outcomes. They understand that in order to find solutions it will require new thinking, creativity, and an entirely different approach in how we fund and manage tomorrow's essential government operations. They understand that regardless of good or bad times, successful leaders must focus on effectiveness. Why? Because effectiveness for leaders mean doing the right things and doing those right things well! They also understand that despite the pressures on government to reduce the total number of the workforce, the types of services offered to residents must be packaged in a manner that best protects their needs. To achieve this, it will require unwavering, dedicated, and strong leadership like never before. It will require women and men who are critical thinkers, who are able to adapt, and who are able to invent and then re-invent systems. Tomorrow's leadership positions will not be for the faint of heart. They will be reserved only for the dedicated professionals who understand the importance of perseverance.

Given the reasons for which fire and police departments were established, public safety will continue to have significant importance and purpose in our nation and throughout the world. The question for this country is: How do we as a nation, state or local community determine its appropriate size and budget allocation? While the answer may be different for each community, to get there, it will require the same approach; new emphasizes being placed on participative styles of managing. It will require providing a seat for all stakeholders at the table and jointly determining the right balance from the bottom up. It will require a complete paradigm shift in staffing formations and services offered. It will require setting aside all partisan, ideological, cultural and religious disagreements and bickering. Ultimately, it will require the emergence of strong leaders.

During my career, irrespective of where we were in the economic ebb and low cycles, I too was committed to being a transformer of the public sector with hopes of making a true difference in each of the departments and communities that I was privileged to serve in. I set many goals. I realized that to achieve them, I would have to promote into positions of authority. Positions that would give me the platform to make the needed changes that I believed would benefit the community and the organization.

Given the tremendous number of talented persons I had worked with over the years, to successfully promote, I believed that I needed to out study others in order to set myself apart from them. In taking this approach during promotional processes, many times I succeeded in my efforts to promote. However, there were several other times that I failed miserably. Each time the failures occurred, I concluded that it was because I had not invested the right amount of time to the proper study of the technical aspects of the job or that I did not have a command of particular rules and regulations of the department.

It was not until I became a captain within the department that I began to develop an entirely different perspective. As an administrative captain, I was often assigned by the department leadership to serve on outside interview panels for other cities. It was during these occasions that I began to observe that people who were technically strong in knowledge and able to recite all aspects of the rules and regulations of that department were seldom the ones being recommended for promotion. In fact, I began noticing that I myself was recommending people for promotions that had entirely different skills than those technically related. As I began observing this outcome more frequently, I became intrigued and began researching just what makes one successful in an interview setting. As I continued to promote, I also began requesting to serve on interview panels so that I could continue studying and researching this rather vexing question. I would carefully study the manner in which participants articulated beliefs, their presentation style, word choices, their body language, and the qualitative impact of nervous habits being exhibited. In addition, I took notice of the specific qualities that panelist considered impressive in a candidate, especially those that lead them to make their recommendation.

Over time, it became clear to me that virtually everything I had previously learned about how to prepare for an interview was completely wrong. It was not the person who knew or retained the most technical information. It was not the articulation of how one would carry out their duties in the position. It was not necessarily the person with the longest tenure or experience in a particular position. It was a combination of very specific factors that we can each learn, control and manage.

As you read each chapter of this book, I want you to view them as building blocks that when integrated, create a pathway to the ultimate achievement of your goal. Few books, if any, have ever discussed just how critical each building block is to one another. However, you will find that they are interdependent. What I have come to finally realize is that many of those who have succeeded have done so using virtually every one of these building blocks. Some did so while consciously aware of the power of each block. Others did so by intuitively applying each. They can speak to some of them but, without realizing it, are also engaged in the others.

As you begin incorporating each component into a daily practice, you will have successfully created a comprehensive systems approach to success. It is the same systems approach used by the most successful.

You will also find that the true power of these integrated building blocks are best demonstrated in interview settings.

As you know, during an interview, you must articulate your core values, share your experience and creative ideas, and in an organized and crystal clear manner, demonstrate your technical abilities, while simultaneously exhibiting energy, leadership abilities, and great interpersonal skills and passion for your profession as you enthusiastically establish an instantaneous bond with the panel—all within a specified period of time!

All of this is actually achievable if you are willing to put forth the required time to master and practice the suggested concepts within this book. The even better news is that after putting in the work, it will immediately begin to catapult you above all other potential candidates.

Why? It is because most candidates fail to apply the necessary time to this critical phase of the hiring or promotional process. Most improperly plan and prepare for these interactions. In fact, many will put forth more effort filling out their submitted application and resume, than they will for the interview. When candidates fail to properly prepare, they misread or completely miss the many dynamics that are occurring right before their eyes as they go through the interview process. Some become completely absorbed in their fear. Many others try so hard to convince the interviewers of their abilities that they forget to manage the process and fail to fully respond to questions being posed to them. Consequently, their verbal and non-verbal responses begin to conflict with one another leaving the panel feeling disappointed and confused.

The simple truth is that for one to have a powerful interview, it will require you to demonstrate substance, ability and confidence. Each one of these attributes can be demonstrated if you carefully plan and prepare in advance of an interview. Yet, even with this knowledge, it has been suggested that less than five percent of those preparing for upward mobility in any profession are willing to put forth the necessary time and attention to achieve desired results.

Someone once aptly stated, "we are all capable of high achievement, but only the successful will admit to it!" Stated differently, only the successful are willing to pay careful attention to the detail and special nuisances that make one stand out above others. They prepare by carefully studying and understanding past issues and trends within the city and department they hope to join and lead. They stay abreast of their industry trends and directions of their profession. They broaden their reading to include issues outside of their industry so that it not only broadens their knowledge base, but it also provides them with an endless reservoir to draw from when considering creative ways in addressing problems. Then, considering past and futuristic trends within and outside of their industry, they are able to make educated projections about how a community can best position itself to meet the needs of the future. They carefully develop a plan that reflects the industry trends, while also tailoring it to factor in the current culture of the city and department so that neither is shocked or resistive to the change. They develop meaningful strategies to ensure that the City and the Department are in a position to benefit from these predictive possibilities derived from the trends. And then, unlike most, they develop strategies about how to articulate these insights and possibilities in the interview process. Through proper preparation, they essentially help the panel to embrace their vision by painting, through the use of carefully chosen words, massive results in advance! Successful chiefs also understand the importance of preparing both mentally and physically in advance of their interview. Through the development of a wellness and interview strategy, you too will become unbeatable!

Regardless of whether you are a chief of the department who is ready to take on a larger department, a deputy or assistant chief who is ready to lead your own department or an entry level police officer or firefighter, your decision to read this book and begin applying the recommended strategies and building blocks will immediately move you into that five percent of persons who routinely commit to taking the necessary steps to ensure their future success!

In utilizing these concepts and strategies, you will be quite amazed at how quickly you will begin to take control of your career path. No more wishing and hoping, just careful planning, execution and succeeding. This will not be a magical occurrence. It will occur because you, like all other successful people, are willing to dream, develop goals, prepare action plans, and execute your strategies. Just as you will soon find, it is the belief and investment in themselves that allow the most successful to reach the top of their profession. They turn dreams into reality as opposed to simply daydreaming.

Let me welcome you to that top five percentile as you initiate your journey and begin "Reaching for the Gold" in your chosen profession!

Now, let's go to work!

*"It's an unusual person whose desire is larger than his/her distaste for the work involved."*

*Earl Nightingale*

# Objective of this Book

It's important to state at the outset that the objective of this book is to serve as a practical guide to assist you in identifying, organizing, honing, and ultimately packaging your unique skills and strengths into a format that will demonstrate to the panelist and ultimately the appointing authorities, that you are the best person for that top seat!

It shares with you two of the best-kept secrets to a successful career and life. It offers proven methods on how to successfully create such essentials as instantaneous connections with the panel, how to send consistent unified messages through coordinated verbal and non-verbal communication, and the interrelationships of each of these efforts and how they translate into an enhanced "L" factor. It clarifies the true purpose of an interview and the simple, yet often violated rules of an interview.

What this book is not intended to be is a substitute for having gained technical and broad based substantive knowledge of your industry. I would not recommend incorporating these concepts as an alternative to having carefully studied the history of the public safety profession and trends that assist in predicting its future. Nor is it intended to serve as a substitute for failing to stay abreast of the many industry changes taking place around the world today. In other words, this book is not for the lazy or shallow minded. It should not be perceived as a "CliffsNotes" route to the achievement of success.

For those who choose to engage in the often used strategy of "faking it—in hopes of one day making it", I encourage you to close this book now and return it to its place of purchase.

History teaches us that there is a price we each must be willing to pay for the achievement of success in our life. It includes the setting of goals, comprehensive planning, and the taking of action, belief, hard work, sacrifice and perseverance. Nothing can or should ever replace these time tested and proven formulas.

*"Happy are those that dream dreams and are ready to pay the price to make them come true."*

*Leon Joseph Suenens*

# Turning Dreams into Reality: The Magic of Goal Setting

Beginning at a very young age, we each grow up with the excitement and enthusiasm of one day achieving our dreams. We spend countless hours pondering what we want to become or hope to obtain in our lifetime. Many of us have invested several hours, months and even years, daydreaming about how wonderful it would be to live out our desires. Yet, despite all of the time invested in our dreams, despite all of our sincerity and excitement of the possibilities, only a very small percentage of people are successful in transforming their dreams into reality. Why is this? Psychologists have posited several reasons, including such interventions as environmental influences that gradually move us away from our dreams. One such environmental influence is that of conformity. Based on the environment in which we grow up, we tend to take on the same behaviors as those of the majority. If the majority appears satisfied with a high school degree, an eight to five job, an apartment or cozy bungalow home, we tend to feel that it is a normal and acceptable life. For many, it is.

In other situations, we can encounter negativity as we begin sharing our career dreams with others. Without hesitation they will tell us how foolish such thoughts are and that we do not possess the skills, background, education, or connections to get there. Before long, we too begin believing the same and soon thereafter, settle for what we have.

Then there are those who secretly harbor fears about the possibility of failure or who simply do not believe that they have what it takes to put forth the hard work involved in achieving their dream. In this situation, we become our own worst enemy.

Finally, there are those who have convinced themselves that the time necessary to achieve such a desire is too great a commitment and investment. Never mind the reality that the time will pass whether they commit to the effort or not. They become willing to allow their careers to go in whatever direction circumstances might take them.

However, this is not the behavior of the successful. Successful people do not subscribe to the belief that it is based on who you know or how well connected you are. Deep within their heart, they know that they can obtain their desired dreams if they commit to doing certain things. They recognize that it will not happen overnight, but with an unwavering commitment to their dream, they are destined to achieve it. These are the people who continuously focus on their dreams, thinking of them every morning when they awake, throughout each day and as the last thought each night before falling asleep. Whether intuitively or taught at an early age, the highly successful understand that there are two well kept secrets required of each of us in order to successfully achieve our life and career dreams.

The first well kept secret comes as no surprise. You must first decide on your desired dream. But after doing so, where most fall woefully short is to then begin to clearly articulate why that dream is so important to you? After you are clear as to why your goals are so important to you, then and only then, should you begin identifying the necessary actions to be taken in order to achieve them? Not just any action, but a well thought-out, written plan of action steps that when followed, moves you closer to realizing your ultimate dream. You see dreams are actually goals we choose to set for our lives and career. Without goals, and the reasons for which they are so important to us, we have little if any motivation to proceed. The action steps are objectives. Without developing action steps that lead us toward our goal, we are in essence, without direction. We become the proverbial rudderless ship casting about roaring waters with no idea as to where we may end up with our life and career.

You have now decided that you want to be the "Chief of Department." Until now, you may not have done much more than dream about this possibility. Make no mistake about it; this truly is a great start. By taking this first important step to decide where you want to take your career, you have initiated an important process within your subconscious mind. But to continue traveling up the successful path of transformation, it now requires an investment of time and effort. This unfortunately is the point in which most people will stop. But for people like you, it is the time to ask yourself that very important next question: Why is this goal so important to me?

What are your reasons for this decision? Knowing what you want out of life is essential. However, to be able to pursue it with vigor, we must have well-defined reasons as to why it is so important to us. In fact, the more reasons for which you desire to ascend to that top position, the greater the probability of your success. Is it because you love the challenge inherent in the position? Is it the prestige or the responsibility of the position? Is it because of the enhanced lifestyle that comes with a larger income or the notoriety given the stature of the position? Is it because you have great ideas in how to better this profession? Do you have strong leadership skills that when applied will move your chosen profession into an entirely new and more positive direction? Could it be that through your leadership, you will provide an even greater safety net to the residents of the community you serve? Could it be that through your stewardship you will provide a better way of developing and caring for the members of the department? Perhaps it is due to all of these reasons.

Once you have clarified specifically what makes this goal so important that you are willing to sacrifice the time and energy necessary to achieve it, begin writing them down. As a practice, always carry a copy with you. Begin reading them several times each day. This one simple act will begin providing you with several benefits. Your reasons will serve as the basis for keeping you motivated as you begin enjoying incremental successes. They will also sustain you during times in which you experience occasional setbacks in your journey. Most importantly, you will begin imprinting into your subconscious mind your desires, allowing it to go to work on the achievement of your goal.

Once you have defined your reasons for this goal, it is important to then begin preparing an action plan that addresses the objectives you will need to achieve in order for the goal to be realized.

Objectives are the "how to" in achieving your goal. What are the pre-requisites to becoming chief of the department in the town, city, county or special district in which you currently reside? What are the "minimum" and "highly desired" educational prerequisites? What are the prior experiences and background that is required? What seemed to be the characteristics and traits that were most attractive to that community when they last selected a Chief for their community? Do you presently posses any of these requirements, characteristics or traits?

Begin identifying any gaps in your background. Whether it is experience, education or specific assignments, begin writing out objectives to define how you will acquire them. Be extremely specific in this exercise. If you need an Undergraduate or Masters Degree to meet the prerequisites for the position, even if it is listed as highly desired, you will want to begin reviewing educational programs available to you now. Based on when such programs are available, begin identifying the dates by which you will apply for each class. Develop a master schedule reflecting the month and date by which you will complete each required course to ultimately achieve a Undergraduate or Post Graduate degree. Do the same with respect to special assignments or experiences. Depending on the size of the department you are currently a member of, requesting to be assigned to a particular division or function may not be as simple. In these circumstances, don't be afraid to consult with the current Chief and ask that you be allowed to volunteer in the position a few hours a week in order to gain experience until an opening occurs. Be mindful of the FLSA rules in your organization. Some departments may reject such a request for fear of having to possibly compensate you for the work, even though it was voluntary. In these situations, call your Human Resources (HR) Director and seek advice.

If you are currently one of two or more deputy or assistant chiefs, ask the chief if you can be assigned to manage those areas that will allow you to gain additional experience in the areas you currently lack. If you are the Chief of a smaller department and you have a goal of managing a larger department, ask the Town Manager, City Manager or Mayor for the opportunity to work on special projects outside of the department so that you can gain more experience and understanding in managing on a larger scale.

By clearly stating your goal, identifying reasons for which they are important to you, the benefits that you, your family and others will realize as a result of your having achieved them, and then outlining the specific steps necessary to achieve each objective, including dates by which you will complete each, you will become part of a very small percentage of people who have begun the process of ensuring success. You will have moved from simply dreaming to actually transforming your dream into a reality.

By engaging in these efforts, you are now causing three things to happen. As stated earlier, you will start by imprinting into your subconscious mind your desires in very vivid and specific terms—why it is so important for you to succeed. This clarity allows the subconscious mind to move you in the proper direction as it seeks out opportunities to succeed. Second, it gives you a written plan of action from which to work. With such a plan, you can navigate through even the toughest of times as you move toward your goal. Third, it will allow you to focus your time and energy specifically in those areas that bring you closer to the achievement of your goal, thus removing guesswork, wasted energy and missteps. Each of these efforts will immediately begin to catapult you above the vast majority of people who simply dream and fail to take action!

### *Integrating Personal and Professional Goals*
Like so many others, early in my career, I found myself constantly struggling to balance my personal life with that of my professional goals. While working on my graduate degree or on those many evenings I would work late, I found myself feeling guilty about the amount of time I was spending away from home. However, whenever I spent time with my family, especially while traveling with our kids who played on highly competitive soccer teams, I would feel equally guilty about not focusing my attention on key projects I was in charge of or on the further development of my professional career.

I later learned that the two goals did not have to be mutually exclusive. What I failed to understand in the beginning is that you must develop your personal and professional goals and then align them. They cannot successively be compartmentalized and expected to work as planned. If you have family or a significant other, sit down with them prior to finalizing your professional goals and discuss your plans in detail. Seek agreement on the ways in which you can best balance their needs with your professional goals. Openly discuss the short and long term benefits of achieving both. By establishing a mutual understanding, you will find that you can let go of the guilty feelings and fully enjoy your time at work or play. During this effort, remember to build in a small amount of flexibility. Having the ability to adjust schedules during those occasions when unexpected conflicts surface is also important.

### *Establishing and accomplishing your goals:*

- State your goals using action oriented positive words.
- Make sure that your goals are exciting, yet realistic.
- Make sure that each goal causes you to stretch.
- Keep them to a one to three year horizon so that they are in reach and sight.
- Carefully prioritize each goal.
- Be specific about each objective.
- Include completion dates for each.
- Balance your professional goals with your life needs.
- Include your family or significant other early in the planning process.
- Monitor and assess your progress on a monthly basis.
- Update them as situations and achievements occur.
- Keep your professional goals to yourself, family and only those with similar goals (more about this later).

*"The greatest discovery of my generation was that human beings can alter their lives by altering their attitudes of mind."*

*William James*

# The Power and Benefit of Maintaining A Positive Attitude

Each day, we read in the newspaper or hear on the news about a person who was considered disadvantaged in life having grown up in abject poverty, raised in several foster care homes or had severe learning or physical disabilities. Yet, regardless of the perceived shortcomings that others may have assigned to them, they succeeded in achieving their goals.

We have each experienced some level of unexpected struggle and challenge in our lives. It is a part of life and no living being is allowed to escape it. Yet, despite such impediments, some appear much more capable of finding the necessary strength and resolve to push through these struggles and challenges in pursuit of their goal. Conversely, many others seem willing to allow similar types of adversity they have encountered or were born with to serve as justification for giving up or quitting.

What is the reason for which some people seem to push through and succeed despite their challenges while others become paralyzed and give up?

The answer serves as the second well-kept secret to a successful life and career—It is our attitude. It is the belief and feelings we have about ourselves, those around us, and about life itself, that makes the difference. Irrespective of our background, our ethnicity, gender, nationality, or the circumstances we are confronted with, if we establish a goal that is worthy of our pursuit and we adopt a positive mental attitude, there is virtually nothing on this earth that can stop us from one day achieving it!

As defined by the Business dictionary, Attitude is "*a predisposition or a tendency to respond positively or negatively towards a certain idea, object, person, or situation. Attitude influences an individual's choice of action, and responses to challenges, incentives, and rewards.*"

A positive attitude provides us with optimism and it eliminates the negative thinking that most people engage in on a daily basis. It promotes healthy self-esteem and confidence, and it causes us to expect to succeed in our objectives thus leading us to our ultimate goals.

Even in the face of difficulty, it is this optimism that reminds us that our current situation will not last forever. If we stick with it, circumstances must and will soon change! That is because a positive attitude motivates us to look for solutions, to be creative, and to always be willing to persevere. With a positive attitude, we are much more happier in our life and in our work. We maintain more energy. We possess broader perspectives and can more readily identify opportunity. People enjoy being around us because we inspire not only ourselves, but them as well.

Many years ago, Harvard University conducted a study to identify the key traits that made one successful in their career. Of those they studied, they found that eighty five percent reached the top of their chosen profession in large part because of their attitude and fifteen percent because of their aptitude!

Other studies have confirmed that over time a poor attitude can cause us to become self-fulfilling disasters. It is also important to understand that attitudes are the reflection of a person's internal perspectives. What we believe on the inside (especially how we feel about ourselves) is continuously reflected on the outside by our behavior and word choices.

It also manifests itself in our body language. Those with poor attitudes tend to slouch more, maintain closed body positions and frown more than others.

While poor attitudes can have a powerful negative effect on our behavior, the good news is that attitudes are not set in stone. The very same influences that lead to the negative attitude formation can also create change.

So just how can we begin improving our attitude? Experts suggest that we begin by immediately behaving as though you already have a healthy positive expectant attitude. Our actions directly affect our feelings and it is our feelings that trigger our daily actions! To change or improve on our attitude, we must first mentally become the person we want to become. We must choose to be optimistic. We must learn to seek the potential bright side often embedded in difficult situations we are confronted with. We should also read inspirational stories and quotes as often as possible. In addition, we should limit our interactions with negative minded people and try instead to associate with positive persons. Remember, through continual associations, both behaviors are very contagious.

When dealing with your peers and especially your subordinates, remember the words of Andrew Carnegie. At one point in time, he was said to have more millionaires on his payroll than any other company of similar size in the United States. When asked how he attracted so many people with such economic wealth, he allegedly replied that they were not all millionaires when he hired them. He was then asked how he managed to develop so many people into millionaires. He responded by saying, "Developing people is a lot like mining for gold. You can move tons of dirt and you may only find a few ounces of gold. But you don't go looking for the dirt—you go looking for the gold!"

Research shows that people with positive mental attitudes take the time to find the best in others. They do not focus solely on ones shortcomings. They help to develop and assist them in reaching their highest potential.

There are four components that make up our attitudes:

- Confidence
- Expectations
- Adaptability
- Appreciation

Understanding the significance of and incorporating each of these four elements into your daily activity will well position you in your next interview process and in your life.

And always remember the words of the famous motivational speaker Zig Ziglar. He stated it best when he said, "It is our attitude that determines our altitude in life!"

*"Our subconscious minds have no sense of humor, play no jokes and cannot tell the difference between reality and an imagined thought or image. What we continually think about eventually will manifest in our lives."*

*Robert Collier*

# OUR SUBCONSCIOUS MIND AND CENTRAL NERVOUS SYSTEM: FRIEND OR FOE?

Scientists have confirmed that our subconscious mind and central nervous system are incapable of discerning between an actual experience and the same experience that is imagined in complete detail. If we were to imagine something in vivid detail, our subconscious mind and central nervous system will view this imagined event as though it had actually occurred. What if, in anticipation of an important upcoming event such as an interview, we were to begin worrying about possible negative outcomes by imagining all the things that could go wrong? In doing so, we could literally create the negative mental, emotional and even physical body responses to an event that hasn't even happened. In these instances, we could suffer just as much or even more, had the focus of our worry actually occurred.

Research suggests that the imagined occurrence can cause us to feel as much as ten times worse. Further, the person who finds him or herself going through such an intense, worrisome experience of failure can bring about the same physical symptoms of those going through the actual failure. They can experience such symptoms as anxiety, humiliation, headaches and queasiness. As far as our mind, nervous system and now our body are concerned, we have failed before the event has actually occurred. If we continue to worry in this fashion, visualizing the failure in detail, we can bring about the exact outcome during the actual interview.

If you have ever played a round of golf, you may have experienced the following for yourself. How many times have you watched a person address their ball on a water hole and say, "I hope I don't hit it in the water." Then, like magic, into the water it goes! I have friends who have perfected this problem by including "water balls" in their golf bag! Each time they come to a hole that has a water hazard, they have pre-determined where it will most likely go, so they tee up a cheap or damaged ball that they won't mind losing to the water gods. Our subconscious mind and central nervous system are so powerful that when we improperly use them, they proceed to create the very circumstances we fear most.

I offer this additional example as one given to me several years ago. If I were to place a plank that is twenty five feet long and twelve inches wide on the ground and offer to give you $100.00 dollars if stand on it and walk from one end to the other without touching the ground. Would you do it? Of course! In fact, you would probably feel so confident about your ability to achieve this request you would probably include a perorate as you skip toward the other end to collect your money. Now, suppose I take the same plank and straddle it on top of two buildings that are 200 feet tall. However, this time, I place a thousand dollar bill at the end of the plank and ask you to return tomorrow morning to walk across the plank and collect your reward. I am certain that with this change in height you would be thinking primarily about why it is you should not do it. Throughout the evening your fear could become the dominant thought. You forget about the reward and begin focusing your attention on the consequences of failure. Most would begin having thoughts about what would happen if they lost their balance or fell 200 feet to the ground and severely injured themselves. After thinking intensely about the possibility of losing your footing and falling, you may begin feeling extremely nervous. You may begin perspiring. If you do chose to try it, chances are, you would now create the exact failure that you so intensely imaged. By tightening up your muscles and being focused on the potential for falling as oppose to the joy of success, in all probability, you will fulfill exactly what the subconscious and central nervous system has already assumed happened. All of these reactions occur out of the fear that has now been imprinted in your subconscious mind and central nervous system.

Although these systems can be destructive to us, the opposite is also true. We can utilize them to our advantage. We can program them to achieve the success we seek as well. This is because these two powerful systems only act on the information that we feed them. They are neutral until we provide them with data by which they begin to act on. Just as the persons who unwittingly focus on failure can ultimately defeat themselves, we can use the exact same forces to our advantage and successfully achieve our objectives.

This is precisely why a positive attitude becomes so crucial to ones ultimate success. Remember, our attitude is made up of four characteristics. All four are very important to our well being. However, two in particular are essential to the programming of our subconscious mind and nervous system: confidence and expectations. Maintaining confidence and having an expectation of succeeding in your objectives and goals are essential to the proper programming of these two powerful systems.

*"Our goals can only be reached through a vehicle of a plan, in which we must fervently believe, and upon which we must vigorously act. There is no other route to success."*

*Pablo Picasso*

# Developing a Vision Based Strategic Plan and Playbook

In both the public and private sector, strategic plans, business plans and actions plans are all essential tools for organizational vitality and success. If we want to succeed in achieving our personal goals, such well thought-out plans and the development of specific action steps are equally important for people as well. Yet study after study shows that less than five percent of the population involve themselves in such planning efforts. Less than five percent will sit down, invest time beyond that of a well meaning daydream and give thoughtful consideration to why their dreams are important to them. They will fail to give consideration to what it will take to bring their goal to fruition and then develop a written plan that they can follow and track their progress. Remember, the missing elements that prevent most people with a dream from fulfilling it is their unwillingness to understand why it is important to them, develop a well thought out plan, and then proceed to take action.

Over the years, I have made it a habit to purposefully ask up and coming officers the following questions:

- What are your career goals?
- Can you define your values in thirty seconds or less?

- Do you know where that bright line is in your life that you refuse to cross personally or professionally? Does it apply only when you are being observed publically or does it also apply when you are alone?
- Have you conducted an inventory of yourself to identify what your greatest strengths and weaknesses are? Can you state them to me?
- Have you given thought to how to maximize on your identified strengths, while also developing strategies for the elimination of the weaknesses that could very easily be what is holding you back?

These are a few of the fundamental types of questions the best businesses of the world spend thousands of hours clarifying to ensure they position themselves for maximum success in the marketplace. They are the same basic questions that we must be willing to ask ourselves as well. Then, we must take the answers and devise a written plan that we can follow and measure our progress.

The Business Dictionary defines Strategic Planning as the *"Systematic process of envisioning a desired future, and translating that vision into broadly defined goals or objectives and a sequence of steps to achieve them".* As we know, strategic planning begins with the desired results and works backward to current status.

There are many approaches that you can take in developing a plan. I am recommending the use of a basic Vision Based approach. It will allow you to take your vision of Chief of the Department and work backwards to where you are today. This format will also help you in defining your purpose, the values that you stand for, identify your strengths and weaknesses, and then allow you to outline objectives for enhancing those strengths and eliminating the weaknesses.

By combining the playbook portion with your vision based strategic plan, you are incorporating your personal game plan. Just as in sports, a game plan assists in getting you ready for the actual game. It is a carefully prepared plan that identifies data that will be essential to your success. It also lays out your strategy in the interview process and based on the collected data, helps you to understand macro and micro issues effecting the city and department. With this understanding, you can then anticipate various types of situations and questions that will likely come up during the interview.

As an example, during your data review, you find that the City is struggling to retain major businesses in their jurisdiction. This will most likely have a negative impact on their revenue stream. The questions you must seek answers to include why they are leaving? Is it because of crime, high taxes, or regulatory restrictions? Each answer will allow you to anticipate probable questions that the panel may ask you as they seek candidates who can assist them in solving critical problems they are experiencing. You can now consider your best responses for potential questions well in advance of the interview.

Also, the playbook portion should include daily and weekly practice schedules to assist you in internalizing your developed responses. This will allow you the ability to express your thoughts in an energetic and persuasive manner during the interview. The scheduling of activities will keep you on track. Continual improvement ultimately brings you closer to the achievement of your goal.

No matter where you are in your career, it is never too early or too late to develop your personal vision based strategic plan. However, the playbook portion becomes relevant only after you have identified a particular position or department of interest.

The development of a good strategy relies solely on your ability to identify key, relevant issues occurring in the department, city, state and federal levels. It will directly affect the strength of your strategy so be diligent and as thorough as possible. Go only to reliable sources in seeking data. Never hesitate to ask as many questions as necessary to get data. In answering the elements of a personal plan, it forces us to begin thinking about who and what we stand for in our personal and professional life. What do we really want from our career and why? We begin to assess our strengths and identify weaknesses. We can begin formulating possible strategies for addressing areas of need, such as formal education. We collect useful data that will allow us to speak with depth during the interview. Such planning will greatly assist you in charting and securing your future. By going through these assessments, you will also be in a stronger position during the interview to respond to questions because you have taken the necessary time to give careful and sincere thought to various areas and your answers become more powerful, personal, authentic, substantive, and meaningful.

The general elements of your Vision Based Strategic Plan and Playbook should allow you to comprehensively answer four critical questions. They are:

- What special qualities do I currently possess?
- What is it that I want to ultimately accomplish?
- What are the best ways of my getting there?
- Who are the persons that could assist me in my endeavors?

By answering these questions in detail, it will cause you to include at minimum, the following categories.

### Your Mission Statement

A mission statement is a declaration of your core purpose. What in your view is your purpose on this earth? What drives you? This is not intended to send you off in search of the meaning of life, but more importantly for you to understand when your life on earth ends, what do you want it to have stood for? Based on your actions, how will your family and friends define your life? Will it be consistent with what you devoted yourself too? In seeking an answer to this question, try going to sources of inspiration personal to you. This could include such religious sources as the Bible, Talmud or Quran. It could also include writings by great philosophers, poets or authors. Based on your personal belief system answer this question for you. By clarifying your purpose, it directs your actions and behaviors so that they are consistent and in alignment with one another. By bringing your outward behavior and daily actions in complete alignment with that of your purpose in life, you begin to live in harmony while also letting others know what they can expect from you.

Many years ago, Dr. Charles Garfield, an expert in peak performance, interviewed persons participating with him on the NASA Apollo project. What he found was that people with a mission that they believed in were incredibly more productive than those without one.

In a brief written statement to yourself, explain your purpose for your life while on earth.

### Vision Statement

Your vision statement serves as a declaration of where you are headed. It defines your desired future state. A vision statement serves as your "North Star". It is a reminder to you that over time your daily work will ultimately contribute to the desired destiny. You have decided that you want to become chief of department!

Therefore your vision is the ambitious future Point B to your current Point A. It should be written in a succinct inspirational manner and read regularly. This will provide you with the necessary encouragement to remain focused on what's important.

### Values Statement

Values are the foundational beliefs by which we live our lives. We have all met people who are willing to adjust or set their professed values aside momentarily to get a certain need met. Such individuals are referred to as not having a true core because they stand for nothing. Having an unwavering commitment to our stated values is critical to our self worth and esteem. It allows us to be more productive in work and happy in life. In the late 1980's, Dr. Charles Hobbs, a time management specialist, wrote a book entitled "Management Power". In this book he discusses the importance of developing "unifying principles" or what I prefer to call values. He provides a seven-step exercise that allows you to identify and prioritize your highest values. During that same year my staff and I read the book and followed the seven steps as a way to develop our organizational values. Individually, many of us also applied this exercise to our personal lives as well.

Organizationally, the established values were used to manage day-to-day operations. Those of us who applied the process to our personal lives used our established values to make daily decisions outside of the workplace as well. It was a powerful experience and I continue to live my life using the very same values that I established for myself in the 1980's.

You may have values that you subscribe to and are quite happy with them. You may have values, but have never officially declared them as the ones you live by. Nonetheless, I offer Dr. Hobbs life changing exercise to you for consideration and possible use. At minimum you can follow the exercise and put your stated values into written words and include them in your personal Vision Based Strategic Plan and Playbook.

Recognize that this process will most likely require more than one day of dedicated effort. Begin each session by finding time away from all others so that you can give careful thought to what is being asked of you in each step. I recommend that you begin with two sheets of paper. Create a heading at the top of each with one marked "My personal life" and the other as "My professional life".

Step 1:
Ask yourself, what are my most valued priorities in life? What is it that I value more than anything else? As an example on the personal life sheet of paper maybe it is faith, family, integrity, humility or learning. For your professional career, maybe it is leadership, loyalty, people, training, work ethics or excellence. Whatever they are, list out all of those that are most important to you. Make it as comprehensive as possible.

Step 2:
Rewrite each one using active verbs. Using family as an example you could write it as "Love my family". To state leadership with the use of an active verb you could state it as, "Be a leader".

Step 3:
Now ensure that all of the unifying principles (values) are the highest form of truth for you and equally important that they are compatible with one another. Compatibility is key here. Carefully assess whether or not they truly are compatible. If not, they may not be representative of your highest form of truth.

Step 4:
Write a clarifying paragraph expressing exactly what each unifying principle or value mean to you personally.

Step 5:
This is the most important and the most difficult step. You must now prioritize each of these values. There is a very important reason for this. If you have not properly prioritized your values, you can quickly become misaligned creating poor self-esteem, poor self worth and in effect, living your life in conflict with yourself.

Years ago, as an Executive Officer in my organization, I had several divisions that reported to me. One was the Arson Investigation Division. Another was our Employee Assistance Program (EAP). Under EAP, we had what was referred to as a "last chance contract". This is an agreement with any employee who was found to have a substance abuse problem and was under a doctor's care. As part of entering into this program and in lieu of termination, the employee had to remain free of all substances and agree to random drug testing for a specified period of time. One day, EAP notified me that an on-duty firefighter was scheduled for a drug test that day. I assigned the Division Chief in charge of the Arson division to pick the firefighter up from his station and transport him to the hospital for testing. This Division Chief had also developed personal values for his life as well.

While in route to the hospital, the firefighter asked the division chief if he would consider informing my office that he had gone home sick prior to arriving at the station and then allow him to get out of his car. The division chief asked the firefighter if his request meant that he was dirty? The firefighter insisted that he was not. He then stated that he had been reading about drug tests that have come back with false positive findings. He was the only wage earner in his household and could not afford to lose his job if incorrect results were found. The division chief thought momentarily about granting his request out of concern for the employee and his family. He then proceeded to the facility and monitored the test that was conducted. It came back positive and upon receipt of the results, I terminated the firefighter.

The Division Chief came to my office late one evening and explained what had happened during the transport. He confessed that he had given thought to the firefighters request during that morning of the transport. He then shared that his thoughts quickly turned to the commitment he had made to himself regarding his personal values. It was this latter thought that caused him to complete his assignment as directed. One of his highest personal priorities in life is to always live with integrity. Another was to always be loyal to the organization. Imagine if his number one priority was to always protect the women and men under his charge? This is precisely why prioritizing your values is so critical. All decision-making becomes less complicated and you remain in complete alignment with your values.

One year later, the terminated firefighter visited the division chief and thanked him for giving him and his family his life back. He said that had he not been fired, he would never have found the need to seriously confront his addiction.

Step 6:
Take the next several days or weeks if needed to carefully observe and evaluate your daily performance. Are you living or behaving in alignment with each of your stated values? This becomes your moment of truth. It is not the opportunity to change the values so that they comport with your behavior. It is the time to change your behaviors and recognize a change is necessary if you are to live in truth with yourself.

Step 7:
Bring all behavior in complete alignment with your values and beginning today, live with self-unification.

If you commit to living in this manner, from this day forward, you will experience a sense of confidence in doing what is right. Operating with self—unification will also serve as a basis for any decision-making, personally and professionally. These unifying principles or values, as I prefer to call them, will properly guide you throughout your life and career.

In their book, "Built to Last", Porras and Collins researched corporations in answer to the specific question, "What makes the truly exceptional companies different from other companies?" One key finding was that the best companies lead and managed their organizations based on a set of core values that did not change regardless of who was heading the company. Additionally, any critical decisions made had to be in alignment with those core values. This is an essential element to a successful career and life as well.

### Assessment of your Qualities, Strengths and Skills

In the late 1970's, I enrolled in a half day seminar on interviewing techniques. The session was developed and presented by communications specialist and lecturer, Robin R. Ririe. Through that particular seminar, I learned approaches in how to prepare for interviews. There were two exercises that resonated with me. They included assessing your skills and strengths, and preparing an opening and closing statement during the interview. The latter is discussed in a separate chapter. I have modified them over the years; however, both were quite useful to me throughout my career. Begin this assessment by taking another sheet of paper and ask yourself who is the one person that you most admire in this world. See that person in your mind's eye. What are the qualities, skills or strengths that they have? Begin listing each quality, skill or strength until you cannot think of any more. I want you to assemble a minimum of twenty-five attributes of that person. Now prioritize your list beginning with the one you admire most.

Taking a second sheet of paper, begin writing down your greatest attributes. List as many as possible, but you must list at least twenty-five as well. Now prioritize this list. Take the two prioritized lists and place them side-by-side. Begin noting the similarities in the two lists. You see we tend to admire in others those qualities we see or hope to develop in ourselves. Take the top four assets that you listed on the sheet referring to you and confirm to yourself whether or not you believe them to be your greatest assets. Are they beneficial to an organization? If so, why? For example, if one of your identified strengths is that you have excellent diagnostic skills, how can you translate that skill into a benefit for an organization? Take each of the strengths and write out a concise small paragraph about its benefit and use.

As an example: "I have developed excellent diagnostic skills. I have the ability to take extremely complex problems and analyze them layer by layer until I identify the core issue. From this, I am able to develop solutions to not only resolve the issue, but to incorporate necessary changes to minimize future occurrences of this nature." Then write out an example of where and how you used this valuable skill. Now do the same for the remaining three.

### Weaknesses

Something we seldom do is take inventory of any weaknesses we may possess and acknowledge their existence. We all have weaknesses so it should not be something we are ashamed of. It is only by conducting this objective self-assessment that we are then able to begin addressing them.

Being truthful with yourself, list each weakness you possess. Weaknesses could include such things as poor writing, time management or delegation skills. Now define each in a separate paragraph. Next, you want to write a paragraph about how you are working to resolve each weakness. Be explicit.

As an example, a weakness I currently possess is my tendency to approach matters from a big picture perspective. Because of this, occasionally I may overlook detailed information that could be of importance. Recognizing this weakness, I make sure that I assign someone who is detailed oriented to work beside me as I review organizational concerns. Taking this approach, I am able to ensure that important details are properly captured. Additionally, with each effort, I am learning how to refocus my attention so that I too am able to pick up the big picture issues and the important detail myself.

### Professional and Personal Goals and Objectives

Goals are broad based strategies needed to achieve your mission. Objectives are specific, measurable, action oriented, realistic and time-honored strategies that will allow you to achieve your stated goals and vision.

If you are currently Chief of Department in a smaller community and your goal is to manage a larger organization, this should serve as your newly stated professional goal. Take the list you established earlier outlining all the reasons for which this goal is important to you. Carefully review and ensure that it is complete. Remember, the more reasons for which a goal is important for us to pursue, the better. You should now identify what city in particular you are currently interested in. Have they advertised for it? Have you obtained a recruitment brochure? What qualities are they looking for? Does your assessment of your strengths match up with their needs? Do your strengths benefit the organization? What are the prerequisites for the position? Do you meet them? When is the file date? What are the specific objectives you need to achieve and by when? This would include preparation of an application, references, updating resume, etc.

If you are a chief officer who is ready to matriculate to the top seat, the same process applies.

### Collection of Data
Now is also a good time to begin gathering data to develop a profile of the city. At minimum, you will want to gain an understanding in the following categories:

### Charter or General Law Provisions:
### Goal is to fully understand the governing structure

- Look for any uniqueness's listed within it. Look also at any described role for the Chief of Department.
- City organization chart
- Name and assignment of each Executive Staff member

### Financials of the City:
### Goal is to assess its past, present and future stability

- Latest completed outside audits (be sure to also carefully review the management letter)
- Five year forecast
- Current and past two adopted budgets
- Mid year budget adjustments for past two years
- General fund and non-general Revenue and Expenses
- Current debt ratios
- Pension funding ratios

- Upcoming anticipated capital expenses
- Diversity of revenue stream
- General Fund reserves
- Stability of restricted and non-restricted fund balances (if you note a great deal of internal fund transfers and or negative fund balances, this could be a red flag regarding their stability)
- Strategic Plan for the city and its finances

### City's Rating Agency ratings:
### Goal is to understand their credit worthiness

- Last rating review
- Any upgrades or downgrades
- You can go to the websites of Moody's, S&P or Fitch and look for postings on any particular municipality. Look for any write-ups discussing the financial outlook and any potential threats or weaknesses.

### Business Industries located in area:
### Goal is to determine who the industry giants are

- Types of Industries
- The 10 Largest business employers

### Economic Develop Strategy and Plan: Goal is to determine long term strategies to keep community financially Healthy

- How old is plan
- Who is responsible for its implementation
- When was it last updated
- What are the metrics used to measure progress
- What were the last results

### Demographics:
### Goal is to understand the makeup of the municipality and region

- Population size by day and night
- Ethnicity breakdown

- Educational levels of community
- Average age
- Age percentage by category (senior citizens, adult, juvenile)
- Average income
- Latest census (take note of any dramatic plus or minus changes)

*Crime Stats: Goal is to determine types of activity and determine possible drivers of crime*

- Part one crime statistics over five-year period to determine potential trends

*Major Community Hazards and Threats:*
*Goal is to determine hazards and strength of emergency response plans*

- Identify threats by type and location
- Assess all response plans and resources
- Local hospitals

*Community leaders: Goal is to determine influential and informal members as well to develop a potential "go to" persons list*

- Business leaders
- Neighborhood leaders
- Labor representatives

*Elected Officials at all levels of Government:*
*Goal is to know who your elected officials are (or soon will be) and any causes they typically champion.*

- Federal Representatives for this District
- State Representatives
- County Representative
- Elected Council Members
- School Board and Chair
- What are their individual special interests or causes

*Recognized Bargaining Units:*
*Goal is to determine the number of bargaining units within city*

- Bargaining units by name
- President and Vice President
- Number of persons they represent
- Where members are mostly assigned
- Contract terms and duration
- Issues of greatest concern to them
- Is this a union friendly community or is it one that is generally opposed to organized labor

*Department: Goal is to understand funding history, internal issues and community concerns*

- What has been the history of funding the department beyond that of personnel costs
- Five-year history of staffing levels
- Current staffing level
- Breakdown of personnel by gender, ethnicity, average age and tenure
- Average age of equipment and facilities
- Replacement schedules for rolling stock
- Capital budget
- Dispatch system
- Department issues
- Community concerns
- Status and age of communication equipment
- Disciplinary process used
- Copy of MOU
- Number of formal complaints received each year by category
- Number of grievances filed per year
- Timeframe to adjudicate grievances on average
- Assessment of current organizational culture
- Department priorities
- Goals and Objectives
- Value statement
- Mission and Vision statement

- Strategic Plan
- Training regimens, e.g., Title VII
- List of Senior Staff who will be reporting to you
- Organizational chart

After reviewing these initial documents and any additional data points you deem appropriate, ask yourself if there is a general alignment with your findings and your values? If you find discrepancies or issues that may cause you concern, be willing to pass on this particular opportunity. Unless the city is interested in a departure from their past, do not be so driven by the desire to ascend to the top position that you are willing to overlook conflicts between your values and the culture of the city or department. The vast majority of people regret their decision to ignore the obvious conflicts and find they are miserable in the job.

### Collection and Arrangement of Playbook Material

If you have decided to proceed, given what you have learned about the organization thus far, you are now in a position to begin developing probable questions that will most likely be asked by that community based upon their current challenges and needs. As an example, in your research you note that over the past several years, overtime costs for the department has continuously exceeded the budgeted allocation. During the past three years of approved allocated budgets, you also note that the overtime budget has been consistently underfunded based on their actual experience. While this is a lousy way in which some cities choose to present an allegedly proposed balanced budget to council, it nonetheless happens. The mayor or city manager know you will exceed the budget allocation by the end of the fiscal year, but they have probably decided to address it during the mid-year budget review. You have determined that this is indeed their practice. Given this finding, during the interview there is a very high probability that you will be asked questions about controlling and reducing overtime expenses.

List each issue and possible ideas for how to address them. Place them by categories on separate pages in your document. This will allow you to make changes to that specific issue as you obtain more information or develop a stronger response. By placing only one issue and response on each sheet it will also prevent you from having to rewrite other topics that were included on that same page.

Organize your document so that you have a separate section for each set of questions by category. This would include categories such as finance and budget issues; management issues; community issues and department operations. Now begin writing out every possible question and crafting a strong well-stated response, based on the subject matter. Continuously review, improve on and internalize the content in each section. At some point, you will want to go back to each response to ensure that it is carrying your desired thematic message, is reflective of your values, creativity and problem solving capabilities. This will ensure that you are being consistent throughout the entire interview.

One essential piece of data to gather as soon as possible is an understanding of what the city is really wanting in a new leader? Will you be entering as a change agent due to a recent controversy? Are you entering as a stabilizing force? Is it to continue their current course while improving upon specific elements of the department? Is it to provide stronger fiscal oversight? Determine their true need so that you may prepare your strategy for solutions and responses to questions accordingly. Many times, you can simply ask the HR Director or Executive Search Firm. They each have a vested interest in ensuring the right person is hired.

The collection of this data is designed to assist you in demonstrating knowledge through a well-prepared set of responses during the interview. But, it is also a personal plan that will assist you in navigating through the interview and hiring process. It is not a strategic plan that helps to guide and shape the future of the department you are seeking to manage. If asked during the interview about a strategic plan for the department, you need only be able to explain to the panel or hiring authority the process that you would use to create such an organizational plan. Unless you are currently a member of the department and this is a promotional opportunity for you, you want to be careful in your response. You do not want to have the panel think that you have answers without benefit of having first properly assessed the organization. This will come across as having a canned response. To respond, simply say that while you have general thoughts on potential changes based on your current level of knowledge of the community and department, it would be completely inappropriate to make assumptions from outside the organization without first confirming them through observation and conversations with the members of the organization and community. Tell them that the gathering of such critical information would begin shortly after you have joined the City and would be completed within your first six months. It is also important that you explain to the panel that from your perspective, the only way to develop a true strategic plan for the department is to involve the members themselves. Having complete buy in through participation is essential to its success. Tell them that you also recognize that no one person, regardless of how talented he or she may be, have all the best answers to all matters of concern. Say that you are aware that the department has incredibly talented, dedicated and creative men and women and that having each member directly involved in the development process would allow you to produce a dynamic plan. Explain that you want the organization and community to fully benefit from these talents.

### *Panel Compositions*
In addition to the issues you identify in the organization and city, you must also be prepared to appear before any of number of assembled panelist. There are at least six different potential audiences and interests groups you could potentially face in your interview. They include a panel comprised of 1) city managers and chiefs from larger agencies, 2) Community groups comprised of neighborhood leaders, 3) Business groups comprised of local business leaders particularly from the Chamber of Commerce and the Convention and Visitors Bureau, 4) Faith groups representing the various religions and denominations 5) Department heads and assistant city managers or deputy mayors, and 6) The inclusion of union representatives.

The larger the city, the more likely you will appear before multiple groups. The smaller the community, the greater your probability of appearing before one or two assembled panels. In this situation, representatives from one or all of the above six possibilities could be invited to participate.

For planning purposes, you will want to prepare an opening statement that will resonate with all of the groups, but also have very specific comments that are tailored to respond to the concerns of each specific group when you are before them. As an example, the community members may have concerns of recent burglaries that you noted in local papers. Given these occurrences, as a Police Chief candidate, you can state your awareness of these occurrences and explain how one of your strengths and skills will also assist in addressing it. If it is the business community and you have noted car burglaries occurring in the downtown area, mentioning this awareness would be valuable as well. Easily if you state that this would be a priority for you because all in the community benefit when our local businesses are thriving and tourist feel safe when visiting us. Your goal is not to pander, but to demonstrate to them that you have done your homework and understand the importance of low crime stats. For a Fire Chief candidate, it may be emergency preparedness and it's importance to the welfare of a community. Be prepared to give each group a tailored message.

As you go through your data review phase, many of the probable issues that are most likely to be asked will begin to materialize. Although most questions to be asked by the panels will have been developed by the HR department or Executive Search firm, having prepared responses to questions most likely to be posed by each of these groups will have allowed you to construct well thought out responses in advance. Remember, even if you do not have a panel with any of the special interest groups that I listed above, should you see an opening, you can offer it as a response and state it as an important element to the stability of the community.

As an example, maybe business groups are not included, but the economy remains soft in this community. You can take your prepared statement of the importance of working to ensure business areas are safe and tie it to the need to encourage business growth in the community for the purpose of stabilizing the local economy and keeping taxes as low as possible for all. If labor unions were not included, you could still take the prepared statement for labor and tie it to the importance of creating a vibrate organization through the maintenance of a healthy respectful relationship between labor and management. By maintaining flexibility and nimbleness, all collected data will have value. You will be creating multiple options from which to draw from.

### Last Minute Adjustments By Panel

As a standard practice, just before the panel begins the interview process, the list of questions will be carefully reviewed with the panel as a group. After review they are allowed to make any recommended changes to questions or create new ones if there is a compelling reason for it. Then they will be assigned the questions that each will ask the candidates. As long as each candidate is asked the same question and the question itself is relevant to issues within the department or city, HR and the Executive Search Firm representative are likely to allow for the change.

In light of this last minute adjustment, even if they have not asked you a specific question that you have prepared for, remember, you can couple your prepared response with a response to their newly formed question. This will also allow you to gently lead the panel into those areas you would like to take them into. For example, through literature review of local papers, you may find that issues of importance to community groups may include such desires as getting early notification to residents for burglary incidents occurring in their immediate neighborhood. However, during your interview, even though you were prepared, the panel did not ask such a question. You can now incorporate this information into another response and it will most likely cause them to want to follow up with additional questions on this particular topic.

Begin crafting possible responses to each of the categories of interest in written form. Practice incorporating them in your responses to anticipated questions posed to you by the panel with the goal of bringing them into those areas you want them to follow up on. Continue to refine all of your planned responses until they reflect your beliefs and meet with your full approval. Be sure to also continue to monitor the activities in each community to ensure you have up to date information regarding their latest set of concerns.

Again, never think that these efforts may be overkill. Regardless of whether or not a question that you prepared for is ever asked by the panel, you can strategically couple that prepared response with another answer you give. This gives you two advantages: It again shows your knowledge of the communities concerns, and it serves as a way to pull your panel into areas you are prepared for. If it is an area of interest to that targeted group, believe me, they will be most impressed! So there is no waste of time in this approach.

Regardless of the panel makeup, you will want to maintain an overall thematic approach to the interview. Build a common theme around the importance of the three or four skills and strengths you posses. Avoid adding new and different skills based on responses to questions put before you. Continue to reinforce your three to four skills and incorporate their benefit into the responses to relevant questions. Always stay on message. Continuously introducing different skills can cause them to loose track of what you have to offer.

Similar to the preparation of a speech or lesson plan, you want to leave the interviewers remembering key points so that you stand out above others.

As you develop your plan and particularly the playbook portion, realize that it cannot, nor should you want it to be considered complete at any time. While some base data may be assembled in it's entirety, always remain flexible and nimble. Be willing to adjust, recreate and refine information as needed. You will find that you will continue to learn more and more about the community with each passing day as you prepare for your interview.

*"Regardless of age, regardless of position, regardless of the business we happen to be in, all of us need to understand the importance of branding. We are CEOs of our own companies: Me Inc. To be in business today, our most important job is to be head marketer for the brand called You".*

**Tom Peters**

# CREATING AND MARKETING YOUR PERSONAL BRAND

L ike any world-class corporation, developing a brand is essential if you are to effectively distinguish yourself from your competitors. Development of a personal brand is the manner in which you define and differentiate yourself from other candidates throughout your career, as well as during the interview process. Creating a personal brand is not a gimmick nor should it be considered as the latest fad. Tom Peters is believed to be one of the first to introduce the concept of personal branding. Peters presented this concept in an article entitled, "A Brand Called You."

During that period, it is also believed that the primary reason this concept did not become as popular as it deserved, was because many applied a corporate marketing approach when attempting to incorporate the strategy. In doing so, they immediately began questioning one's ability to market a brand without utilizing a marketing firm and budget. Who could have imagined (other than perhaps a visionary such as Tom Peters) that such an explosion of the internet and social media networks like MySpace, LinkedIn, Facebook, Micro Blogs, Twitter and several other applications would soon become available to individuals? With the introduction of such applications, it has virtually evened the playing field, allowing you to successfully launch and manage your brand, just as effectively as any major corporations does today.

### *Why develop a Personal Brand?*

It is important to understand that you are not creating a brand from scratch. We each already possess one. Some are much more defined and positive than others. How people view us based on our work habits, personal ethics, values, even how we dress and comport ourselves each day establishes our personal brand. When we fail to take control of how it is packaged or when we underestimate how everything we do or say contributes to it, our brand can easily become an inhibitor as opposed to an asset. A well-prepared brand allows you to identify, define and distinguish yourself by reflecting in a concise manner who you are, what you stand for, and your purpose in life. It also provides the panelist and hiring authority an understanding of what you will bring to the organization you hope to join. Remember, your ultimate goal is to stand out among all others and in doing so, receive that job offer! Creating or repackaging your personal brand helps to achieve this objective.

If you were to Google your name and city, what would come up? Are you on Facebook, MySpace, or LinkedIn? Will the search be positive or negative? Ironically, if nothing comes up, many will consider you as a non-entity or a weak leader at best. If your name does come up in articles or in reference to LinkedIn, Facebook, MySpace or any other social networking sight, will your brand be consistent in each of these venues? Do they reflect the messaging you would like displayed to the world?

Imagine what would occur if a major corporation were to casually or haphazardly attempt to identify, distinguish or market itself. Imagine what the impact would be if that corporation had several conflicting public images. Imagine if they changed their brand each year. Just how successful do you think they would be in establishing a solid identity and following whenever you heard their name? Which brand would you associate with them? Which would you believe? The outcome would be questionable at best. The same is true of your personal brand. By not taking responsibility for defining and safeguarding who you are and what you stand for (while always ensuring consistency), you are leaving it to others to wonder who you are based on how they perceive you. This is why marketing ourselves to others, letting them know what we stand for and what our strengths are that we can then apply to the betterment of the organization, are so very important. This also allows people the ability to measure and hold us accountable for those traits. But we, not others, should always establish and maintain our personal brand.

So what are the elements of one's personal brand? You have already gone through the self-analysis exercise. The key areas that will greatly assist you are, your mission, vision, values and strengths sections. Now you must begin the process of taking this information and crafting it into a coherent marketing message. Develop it as a half paragraph statement that can be used on your resume, curriculum vitae, articles you pen and as a preferred introduction when you are asked to speak. An important word of warning, once you develop a consistent brand that reflects who you are and what you stand for, you must then begin consistently behaving and operating in that manner. If you consider part of your personal brand as being creative, you must demonstrate that creativity regularly. If you are a dedicated professional, you must reflect those qualities on a daily basis. No one can say they are dedicated professionals if they consistently come to work late, leave early, or provide poor quality work product.

Just as Nike, Disney or Coca Cola markets their products by meticulously reinforcing the elements that make up their brand, you too must market yourself in a manner that meticulously reinforces your key elements. Ultimately, when you participate in the interview you will want the panel and hiring authority to recognize you and your brand as one.

### *Projecting a consistent Message*

Even if people see you differently today than you wish to be portrayed, you can begin to do something about it. On a daily basis, are you comporting yourself in a manner consistent with your preferred brand? Starting today, begin behaving as that preferred person. If you want to be known as a "can do" person, began making sure that you demonstrate your ability and willingness to deliver. Begin demonstrating a belief in your ability to cause things to happen by speaking positively about the possibilities and encouraging others around you to do the same. If you are making a gigantic shift in your behavior, let your peers know. Tell them you have been thinking a great deal about your career and the need to make changes in how you approach things from now on.

Let them know that you are going to approach your duties in this new manner. Explain why you feel these changes are so important for you to do. This will allow them to see the change and speak supportively about it should you ever need them for future references. This also shields you when background checks are initiated and the search firm contacts people you once worked with. It is easier to explain how you changed and why as opposed to explain why others see you in an entirely different way than you are now portraying yourself.

Begin reviewing your personal materials. This should include such information as your resume, curriculum vitae, Facebook page, MySpace page and LinkedIn profile. Is there consistency across all platforms? Do they each highlight those elements you want to be known for? Do you need to begin bringing all of these elements into proper alignment? If the answer is yes, then begin doing it now.

## Blogging

Another very powerful and effective way to establish and market your personal brand is through the marvel of the blog. A blog, short for weblog, allows you to write short commentary to your public safety audience on a website. It gives you an excellent opportunity to write an issue-oriented blog. By framing issues germane to your industry and incorporating wording consistent with your brand, you are achieving two objectives. One is that you are demonstrating your knowledge about the topic and this alone will further your credibility. Second, by having a site where you discuss for example, the importance of being pro-active in this changing environment and the need for strong consistent leadership, it can be quite compelling and would most likely attract a following of readers. This following would also serve to market your name and brand! Creating a blog takes time and thought, but it is well worth the effort. It allows you to take full advantage of the internet's marketing capabilities, as well as highlight who you are and what you stand for!

## Publishing Articles

To begin creating or enhancing your personal brand you will also want to begin submitting articles and comments to your industry magazines, newsletters and any associated periodicals. This allows you to share your message and it gives you yet another opportunity to express your beliefs and reflect your ideas and values. Pick up the phone and call the editor of your trade magazines and ask if they will print an article regarding concerns you have on a particular industry topic? They will typically accommodate you. If they do not, you are at least now on their radar screen for future submittals. Submit letters to the editor in your local newspaper. Write column pieces on the need for your industry to be better partners in the community especially during these times of scarce resources. All of these efforts are powerful tools in helping to establish your personal brand. Just make sure that each article is worded so that it is consistent with your established brand.

Another strategy that provides multiple returns is for you to co-author topical articles with your town manager, city administrator, city manager or mayor. Articles that discuss the ways in which you are reducing costs without negatively effecting service levels, the importance of elevating fire prevention as a community thrust, partnering with police officers on a more meaningful level, ways in which you are developing safety net strategies to protect the community from domestic attacks we are witnessing throughout the country. These are all possibilities that such newsletters as ICMA or NLC enjoy publishing. If you write the article and get your city manager, administrator or mayor to sign it as a co-writer, you are again building your brand and shining a welcomed positive light on him or her and the community as well.

Be creative and consider other ways to enhance your personal brand. When a background check is undertaken, which will also include web searches, you want as much positive, well-managed information about you, your involvement, your leadership and values to pop up as often as possible!

*"Our insecurity comes from not understanding the concept."*

**Plato**

# THE PURPOSE OF AN INTERVIEW AND THE SIMPLE YET UNSPOKEN RULES AND EXPECTATIONS

For many years, I was under the impression that interviews were the perfect setting for both parties (the candidate and hiring entity) to explore whether or not you would serve as a good fit in joining the organization or promoting into a new organizational role. Like many, I considered it a shared opportunity to make this very important determination. Today, I have reached an entirely different point of view. Having found myself in the position of attempting to become chief of department and on the hiring side as a city manager, I eventually came to realize that as a candidate there is only one true reason for which to participate in the interview. That reason is to secure a job offer! From the hiring authority's perspective, the true reason for which they will ultimately make their selection will be to appoint that person who can immediately assist them in solving major issues facing the department and community.

If you have done your research appropriately, you should be able to articulate not only how you will be able to solve those problems, but also the benefit of all the other strengths you will bring to the City. By understanding these two realities, it allows you the ability to approach your preparation phase in an entirely different manner. It allows you to begin thinking more substantively about the organization and city as a whole. You are able to better appreciate what they need and whether or not you have the necessary skill set to offer them. It causes you to begin thinking deeply about important considerations, such as what are the current and future needs of the organization? Can you provide them? What are the constraints in acquiring them? Given these constraints, are there alternative approaches one could take to acquire them? If the approaches are unique, have any other organizations and cities taken such steps? Were they successful? What is the true culture of the department? Are they traditionalist or more of the cutting edge type? Is the internal culture different than the public image being portrayed? Are they transparent, community-oriented or are they insular and protective? Asking and answering questions such as these will cause you to engage in a more in-depth analysis of the department and city. It is in answering these more in-depth considerations that allows you to speak with more substance and less of a need to regurgitate cookie cutter general industry language. It allows you the opportunity to demonstrate that you are the true answer to the hiring authority's needs.

## A Well Developed Process

A properly designed interview process also allows you to intentionally take the lead during portions of the process and allows the panel or hiring entity to take the lead during the remaining portions. Where many candidates fall woefully short is in either failing to take the lead during the times in which they should do so or they falsely assume they should take complete control of the entire interview process. A successful interview will provide you the opportunity to express your ideas, skills, strengths, management style, professional philosophy and any additional responses to the panels' questions while controlling approximately 50 to 55% of the total allocated time of the interview. Assuming a scheduled interview of one hour in duration, this gives the panel members 25 to 30 minutes to ask their questions and pursue follow questions should they desire and it gives you 30 to 35 minutes to respond. If you begin controlling more time than this during the interview, you will be out of balance. In essence, your answers are either too long or you are rambling when giving your response. This is precisely why it is so important to have thought through, developed and practiced responses in advance. It allows you to be concise, complete and focused during the interview.

To ensure that both parties are exploring whether or not this is a potential union in the making, several types of questions are developed and asked during the process. I have found that many candidates are not prepared to provide quality answers to them and others assume that there is some hidden message behind the question. This is because, inwardly, many continue to hold negative views about the purpose of interview processes. Some harbor cynical views as to the actual reasons for its existence. Many consider these processes as a thinly veiled politically correct maneuver to eliminate or "thin the herd out" with the intent of bringing forth persons of their choice. They therefore enter the process with the mindset that they must take control, demonstrate their competitiveness and show the panel why they are wrong. As diabolical as this may sound, believe it or not, there may be rational for such a belief.

According to Dr. Nick Morgan, a communications expert, when people meet for the first time, a non-verbal dance occurs. A dance that is apparently hard wired in each of us and is related to our survival instincts. He states that brain research shows that our bodies send out signals to the other people in the room that fire off unconsciously in our brains. Other people read the emitted signals unconsciously before we are even consciously aware of their presence. He further states that the research suggests our body is attempting to determine whether or not the other persons are friends or foe? If there is no determination, we send out millions of little body signals saying we are braced for a fight. In response, the other person's body will automatically tense up just as fast as yours does.

It provides greater reason for an understanding and appreciation for the actual purpose of the interview. If your mindset is to secure a job offer, the messages your brain sends will be entirely different as you seek the panels support for your cause.

## *The Simple, yet Unstated Rules and Expectations*

It is important to understand that there are several unstated rules of expectations that absolutely must be honored during any interview process. They include:

- Panelists want you to be honest with them. Far too often the panel is left with a feeling that the candidate is attempting to answer a question in the way in which he or she thinks the panel would like to hear it. This only causes the panel members to believe that you are putting on an act and worst, you are patronizing them. The panel and hiring authority see through this behavior 98% of the time. Be yourself and provide them with your personal thoughts and feelings. Be sincere and honest.

- They want you to want the position. Many times, candidates will use words in the interview that suggest that they are unsure as to whether or not they truly want the position. Responses such as, "I will need to give it thought ", or "I need additional information before I can commit" often leave panelists wondering why this person even bothered to apply? This is precisely why I encourage potential candidates to do your homework and decide if this is a position you would be willing to accept if given an opportunity. A lack of a true commitment is a major negative for panelist. Never go into the interview unless you are willing to accept the position.

- They want you to begin by first answering the question being asked of you and then explain the bases for your views.

- They do not expect you to have detailed answers to every question. Remember one of the goals in an interview setting is for them to understand your thinking process and logic. How you would go about seeking solutions to problems is more important to the panel than pretending like you know every textbook answer. If asked a question in which you have little or no experience in, feel confident enough to state that while you have not had experience in that particular type of problem, your practice in seeking solutions to these types of circumstances is to take the following approach. Then explain your process.

- They expect you to listen to the question being asked and not interrupt the panel member or hiring entity while they are posing a question to you. Demonstrate the discipline and courtesy to be patient and await their completion. Interruptions not only reflects the candidates inability to listen, it also causes the panel to believe you are a know it all and rude.

- Never pretend that you understood their question. If you did not, simply ask that they restate it. There is nothing worse than answering a question and having a panel member reply that this is not what he or her was asking.

- Never physically encroach into their space. When standing and speaking to the panelists, maintain 20 to 30 inches apart from them. While seated at the table, never lean into their space or place papers or materials in it.

- Engage all panelists in your discussion when responding to questions. No one likes being ignored during the interview. Creating such an impression causes the individual who felt ignored to begin questioning the reason for which it occurred?

- They do not want you to try and dominate the discussion. On average, you should never speak more than approximately 50 to 55% of the total allocated time during the interview. A major no, no and tremendous irritant for many panelists is to have the candidate launch into 15 minute monologues in response to every question being asked. With the exception of your opening statement, the average response to any question asked should not take longer than 75 to 90 seconds. Much can be explained in that amount of time. Especially if you have a true grasp of the subject matters you are discussing. Some questions may require a bit more time, but remember to always be thorough but succinct. Should the panel want more, they will ask that you expand on your thought. If the interviewing chair has to interrupt you, avoid becoming offended or suddenly losing your enthusiasm. Take ownership of your long windedness and state that you will be more efficient with the use of words in response to their questions. Turn it into a positive. Let them know that you are simply excited about the opportunity and that this position is of great interest to you.

- Display diplomacy and tact throughout the entire interview. In other words, be on your very best behavior.

- Define who you are in a clear, concise manner. For many, not being able to define your style of management or the values used to make daily decisions means you really have not thought much about these important principles. It causes panelists to suddenly lose interest. Remember, they are looking for leaders who know who they are and what they stand for.

- To not assume that you were incorrect with your answer if the panel asks you to further explain or expand on your response. Many times, it is simply to be sure they understood your point.

- Demonstrate your persuasive abilities. Leaders are perceived as having persuasive abilities. If you do not appear to be persuasive with them, how can they expect you to lead the workforce?

At first glance, I am sure that you would agree that each of the above expectations seem like obvious rules for one to follow. However, for varying reasons, even the best-prepared interviewees tend to violate one or more of these expectations during their interview. Oddly enough, a panel member may not even consciously realize why they are turned off by your interview, but when you violate even one of these expectations; the interview can suddenly begin to go downhill. During the Panels wrap up session with staff is when they will begin expressing their gut feelings and concerns regarding the candidate but still not necessarily be able to articulate precisely why they feel the way they do? However, the concerns of whether or not the candidate is a good fit for the position begins to come into question and this concern begins to permeate through to the other panelists.

This is why proper mental preparation, and actual interview practices that are videotaped and carefully critiqued becomes so essential. It provides you with the ability to completely eliminate the subliminal irritants as perceived by panelists during the actual interview process. Reducing as many of these conflicts as possible is what is going to allow you to stand out above all others. If followed, you will ultimately succeed and not be one of those individuals who continue to wonder what went wrong.

*"Clothes do not make the (wo)man"*

*A fallacy for all times!*

# Looking Natty

It is important that I begin this section by first acknowledging that the style of one's clothing is an expression of one's individualism, personality and pocketbook or purse. It is therefore not my intention to attempt to move you away from your individual expressions or cause you to expend additional funds.

More importantly, I recognize that I have absolutely no right to suggest to you how you should dress. I am merely sharing with you the many comments I have received over the years from people throughout the country who have populated the various panels I assembled or the ones I was invited to participate on. This collected information was then combined with research and studies I have reviewed over the years.

What I have found is that the public expects their community leaders to reflect a certain appearance that is consistent with that geographic area's image of Public Safety professionals. Regardless of your personal views, clothing style is based on cultural norms and it does matter. Our attire captures the attention of others. Unfortunately, our style of dress is not neutral. It will leave either a positive or negative impression on those around us. When seen as positive, it begins to establish ones credibility and it enhances our likability before we begin speaking.

Therefore, first impressions are critical. When the panel is viewing you for the first time, they are generally attempting to determine whether or not your style is professional. Do you look like a Chief of Department?

Do you look credible? Do you look like a leader? These subjective determinations are also what cause them to assume you are therefore capable, until you give them reason to think otherwise.

If you are dressed in a flashy, revealing or drab manner, it will be a deterrent for the panel. Forming such opinions about someone based solely on how they are dressed is quite common. Say you are seeking out a new doctor and decide to interview two. Shortly after you saw them, you would immediately begin drawing subjective conclusions. If one was dressed in business attire or a clean well starched white lab coat and the other was wearing a wrinkled Hawaiian shirt and in need of a hair grooming, which one would you proceed with? Without knowing anything about the ability of either doctor, most of us would choose the one dressed in a manner we consider appropriate for that profession.

When considering proper attire for a particular set of circumstances or an upcoming special event, consider reading John Molloy's book entitled, "Dress for Success." Malloy remains one of the leading experts in this field. He later wrote a sequel just for women. Both continue to be quite popular reads. Over the years, he conducted several studies proving that how we dress directly affects the manner in which people perceive and respond to us.

Your selected wardrobe is essential. It represents an important element in the goal to communicate your abilities and it will greatly assist you in being viewed as a confident leader. It can also assist you in creating a bond with the panel as your goal is for them to see you as the right person for the job!

When coaching and assisting persons in how to prepare for their interviews, I always insist that they begin watching two particular Sunday talk shows. One is "Meet the Press" and the other is "Face the Nation". The purpose is not for you to listen and engage in the political debates (although the discussions are usually quite interesting). These shows allow you to observe the verbal and nonverbal communication style of many national and international leaders. Nonverbal includes their body language and style of clothing. The more adept leaders dress in a conservative, professional manner that is also contemporary and designed to compliment one's appearance. I also ask that they pay careful attention to the more mature guest. Take notice of the differences in their dress with that of the younger guests and leaders. They each dress in tasteful, contemporary manners, but the more mature do so without attempting to present themselves in a youthful-looking style.

Your attire can highlight generational differences. This can be a good or bad thing depending on what part of the country you are interviewing in.

If you are a male candidate seeking the top seat of the organization, when in doubt, wear a solid or subtle pinstripe dark business suit with a well coordinated tie. Complete the ensemble by wearing a solid white shirt with pointed collar and dark shoes. For women, wear a solid or subtle pin striped dark colored business suit with pants or skirt that includes a coordinated light colored blouse. Both men and women should always try to take into account the culture of the geographic area you are interviewing in. In many parts of the south or the mid west areas, a thoughtfully selected sports jacket and tie with a bottom down collar and well-coordinated slacks can also be an appropriate choice for men. For women, who are interviewing on the West Coast, particularly in southern California, wearing a trendy pants suit would be quite acceptable. But this particular attire may not be as acceptable in more traditional parts of the country such as in the south. A man from the Washington D.C or New York area may be accustomed to wearing suspenders, cuff links and a pocket square. But wearing them on an interview in a small community in the mid west may leave some feeling that you do not reflect the image of a Chief of Department in their community.

I have had many people take issue with me on this topic. Some have responded that they should be able to wear whatever they choose. Well, in truth, you can. However, it may also mean you won't be recommended for that Chief of Department position you are interested in.

This is why it is so important to gather data regarding the cultural norms of each community you decide to pursue. It will serve as a guide on how to maximize on this very important visual image. Remember, you only get one chance to make a good first impression. Carefully consider your options based on the culture and tradition of that particular community. At minimum, always be aware of it.

In considering your ultimate attire, leave nothing to chance. Carefully select a business suit that is well coordinated with a shirt and tie or blouse. Today, with the many different fabrics and colors available to both men and women, one can be imbued with incredibly dynamic hues.

## <u>MEN</u>

**Suits** are always the best attire. Conservative colors are always safest and provide a look of power and confidence. Consider colors for that particular period of year if you are interviewing in a geographic area that enjoys the four seasons.
Men 60 plus years of age should consider wearing a two button suit jacket. You will want your maturity, which also translates into experience, to come through. Those under 60 can wear up to three button suits. In an interview setting, avoid wearing suits that are made with more than three buttons.

Pocket squares have become more popular today. If you choose to include one, it should be squared across the top and never draping over the pocket. Display just a hint for color, contrast and style.

Label pins should be avoided, unless it is a small U.S. flag or a city pin if this is a promotional interview.

Cuffed pants are quite acceptable. Depending on your body type, you may want to avoid pleats.

Make sure your suit or sports coat and slacks are professionally fitted and adjusted as needed. Whenever in a standing position, you want to always have your jacket buttoned. While seated, unbutton your jacket if it will allow you to feel more comfortable. However, to achieve the best visual appearance while seated, you will want to keep your top button closed. This forms a "V" directing the eyes to your face. While viewing the two shows I referenced earlier, notice that even while seated, the vast majority of quests keep their suit or sports jacket button closed. It will offer the observer a better visual.

**Shirts** should be freshly starched. Make sure collar stays are in collar. White or a pale colored hue is acceptable if you prefer color. Checkered shirts should be avoided.

Wearing a shirt with a pointed collar is always best. Depending on the look you are attempting to achieve, having collar buttons may be appropriate. This is especially true for college towns. If you choose a shirt with French cuffs, make sure cuffs are traditional type and links are subtle and tasteful. Avoid wearing any that sparkle and never wear any that wrap around the cuff. Lastly, avoid wearing cuffs or cuff links with your initials on them. You do not want the panel to think you are infatuated with yourself.

Make sure your shirt is properly fitted. The collar should come together at the very top of collar, forming an upside down V. It should never be separated at the top giving the appearance that it is too tight or too small.

**Ties** should be coordinated with the suit and shirt. Silk material offers a look of quality and sophistication. A standard Windsor knot is preferable. Avoid tie clasps.

A basic rule to remember is that of the three pieces (suit, shirt and tie) only two of the three should have patterns on them. You want to be seen, but you also want to be heard. Avoid creating a busy appearance.

**Jewelry** should be kept to a minimum. I recommend only two pieces of jewelry. Consider wearing only a watch and one ring.

**Shoes** should be professionally polished. Make sure that they are comfortable and compatible with the suit. Lace up shoes should be considered as your preferred choice. Make sure heels are in good shape. Consider having rubber taps put on them. I have witnessed people walk into a room with marble flooring and lose their footing.

**Socks** should be dark in color with no designs. Always wear socks that reach your calf area.

**Hair l**ength and style should be consistent with the standards of the department you are interviewing with. If you use color in your hair, have it done professionally. Consider getting your hair cut a day or two prior to the interview. You want the look of always being well groomed and not appearing as though you just visited your barber specifically for this occasion.

**Mustache:** Always make sure that your top lip can be seen. Do not allow edges of mustache to extend below corners of mouth.

**Cologne** should not be worn. Not only could it possibly be in conflict with the colognes and perfumes worn by panelists, it could also cause a negative reaction if someone is allergic to scents. Also, you never know whether the interview will be held in a small meeting room, which could make a strong scent even more noticeable and possibly offensive.

**Eye Glasses:** If you wear glasses, consider wire frames. Never wear thick or large frames. You want to avoid having them obstruct your eyes and face. Avoid designer frames of all types. Also, make sure that they are properly fitted and adjusted prior to the interview. You will want to avoid having them slide down the bridge of your nose during the interview, causing you to continually push them up while speaking. Also, if you do not have polycarbonate lenses, see your Optometrist. These lenses are thinner and lighter weight. Avoid wearing glasses that adjust automatically in the sunlight. Lastly, never wear tinted lenses during your interview.

**Personal Grooming:** Shave the morning of the interview. Carefully avoid nicks and cuts. If you are nearsighted and wear contact lenses, make sure you shave without them in place. The number of men who completely overlook an unshaved area on their face would surprise you.

Consider getting a manicure and buff, but no clear polish.

## WOMEN

**Suits:** Wearing Business suits with a skirt or pants are both excellent attire for women. Depending on where in the country you are interviewing, skirts versus pants may benefit you more. I would nonetheless encourage woman to select a business suit that you are most comfortable in.

Should you decide to wear a skirt, the length should be based on such factors as time of year and your height and body type. Just above knee is the lowest any shirt should be worn for an interview. During winter months, a skirt below the knee would be an acceptable option.

**Blouse or top** should be coordinated with suit. Avoid wearing low-cut tops. Make sure that all clothing is tailored to fit your body style, height and weight.

**Footwear and stockings**: Wear shoes that are fully or partially closed toe. The heels should never be more than three inches in height. Consider low pumps. Stockings should be skin color and without patterns.

**Scarf's** can be coordinated with entire ensemble. The general rule when mixing and matching clothing for contrast and effect is to only allow patterns to be present on two pieces of your clothing when wearing a scarf. It can be the suit and scarf or the blouse and suit or blouse and scarf. One of the three should be a solid color. You never want your clothing to appear overly busy.

**Jewelry**: Always limit your jewelry and accessories so that they are complimentary, but not overpowering. Either a necklace or chain is acceptable as long as they are not very large. Wear only studded earrings. Never wear hoops or other types of dangling pieces that may cause the panel to be distracted. You want their attention to be on what you have to say and not on something dangling. Finally, wear one watch or bracelet. Always avoid wearing multiple bracelets. Broaches are acceptable, but only if small in size.

**Perfumes and Fragrances:** Do not wear either. Not only could it possibly be in conflict with the colognes and perfumes worn by panelist, it could also cause a negative reaction if someone is allergic to it.

**Nails:** polish should be clear. Nails should not extend too far beyond the tip of your fingers. Longer nails may demonstrate your good care practice, but it can also suggest that you have not been engaged in hands on or strenuous activity. This may not be viewed as valuable for a Chief of Department.

**Purse**: If you choose to carry a purse, it should be small and coordinated with your outfit.

Avoid walking into the interview panel with your hands full. Holding your belonging while attempting to shake hands will be difficult. Set everything down at your place setting before shaking hands.

**Make up**: Minimize use and rely on your natural beauty. Use a foundation to even out skin complexion. Avoid using blush to emphasize or highlight any particular feature. Minimize use of eyeliners and highlights.

**Hair**: Make sure your hairstyle does not cover any part of your face. Also, avoid wearing a style that will cause you to use your hands or flip your head back to remove it from your face while speaking. You want to avoid any distraction.

**Eye Glasses:** If you wear glasses, consider wire frames. You want to avoid having them obstruct your face. Never wear thick or large frames. They hide your face. Avoid designer frames of all types. Also, make sure that they are properly fitted and adjusted prior to the interview. You will want to avoid having them slide down the bridge of your nose during the interview, causing you to continually push them up while speaking. Also, if you do not have polycarbonate lenses, see your Optometrist. These lenses are thinner and lighter weight. Avoid wearing glasses that adjust automatically in the sunlight. Lastly, never wear tinted lenses during your interview.

*"There is no there there."*

*Julia Stein*

# LOCATION, LOCATION, LOCATION!

As City Manager, I was always amazed and disappointed by the number of candidates who arrived late for their scheduled appointment. Despite map tools such as Google, Yahoo, MapQuest, map books, GPS navigation system built into cars and many other similar tools, candidates continue to have to make that dreaded call to inform the panel that they are running late and then must try and explain why? They often respond with excuses that range from the bizarre to the most humble, and virtually every candidate arrived nervous and failed to get on track mentally.

It is extremely difficult to overcome such a mistake. In addition to the candidate being embarrassed, the panelists are left wondering just how serious this candidate is and if he or she is organized enough to take on this important position? Lastly, a candidate's tardiness is viewed as an insult to the panel and hiring authority. It demonstrates a lack of time management and a lack of planning. It reflects quite poorly on the candidate, regardless of how capable she or he may truly be.

What do you do? First of all, avoid being late! If you live in the general area, drive to the location the weekend before so that you are comfortable knowing specifically where the interview will be taking place. Note any roadwork that is taking place. Identify alternative routes and write them down. Factor in the reality that this is a weekend and that chances are greater that weekday traffic will be much heavier. Always plan to arrive at least 25 minutes early so that you can relax in your car and not feel pressured or stressed.

If you are arriving by air, if at all possible, arrive the day before. Rent a car with GPS and do as suggested above. This will also give you the opportunity to drive around the area and gather any last minute information while on the ground.

Should you find that you are going to be late, call and let them know as soon as possible. Always be honest. Using such excuses as "you thought the interview was at 11:00 a.m. as opposed to 10:00 a.m." will not be received as truthful. Let them know where you are and how long you anticipate the delay. Apologize and let them know you would like to continue your plan to get there even if it means you have to wait for another time slot.

Add at least ten minutes of time to your stated estimated time of arrival so that you can sit in your car and gather your thoughts before entering the building. Sincerely apologize to all who are involved in managing the process from the moment you enter the building.

**Check in with the receptionist or HR representative.**
Under normal circumstances, I encourage people to arrive at least 25 minutes prior to the scheduled interview and to check in with the receptionist 15 minutes prior to your scheduled time. This gives you at least 10 minutes to gather your thoughts. Empty your pockets or purse of loose change, cell phone and excess keys before you exit your vehicle. Arriving 25 minutes ahead of schedule also gives you the opportunity to use the restroom or do any last minute adjustments to your hair, makeup and clothing. This provides you with 15 minutes to meet with the Executive Search Firm Representative, the HR Director or their assigned staff member. You never want to check in more than 15 minutes before your scheduled interview. Sitting in the waiting area longer than that can cause you and everyone else to feel uncomfortable.

If you are arriving later than originally scheduled, make sure to first fully gather yourself and visit the restroom before checking in. Once you enter the interview room, let the panel know that this mistake is in no way representative of you. Apologize one final time and then let it go and begin your interview.

*"To be prepared is half the victory"*.

*Miguel De Cervantes*

# THE SEVEN IMPORTANT PHASES OF AN INTERVIEW

Most candidates fail to realize that the actual beginning of any interview process begins when you exit your vehicle in the parking lot and enter the building where the interview will take place. The number of people who have arrived at the designated location and appeared disorganized, nervous or unpleasant when entering the building and approaching the receptionist or person assigned to greet them has always amazed me. I know this because in every city that I have served as City Manager, whether asked or not, staff have seen the candidate as they enter the building and reported their observations back to me or to my senior staff. In most settings, someone will be assigned to look out for your arrival. So, remember, at least one person will be able to report back any incidents or unusual observations involving you. If there is an assigned person to greet you, they will direct you into a holding area as a means of protecting your identity until it is time for the interview.

Most cities or counties are able to withhold your name during this phase of the process until you are considered a finalist. However, in some states such as Florida, it is a requirement under the Public records Act to release such information early in the process. Therefore your identity will most likely be well known.

Regardless of the circumstances, it is imperative that you realize that phase one of the interview process begins the moment you exit your car and begin walking into the building. So from the time you exit your vehicle, it is important that you project enthusiasm, confidence, and energy. Before I discuss the other six phases and their relevance, let me share an actual occurrence that demonstrates this point.

I was being recruited to serve as City Manager of a very prestigious community. I was still employed with another City, but had an interest in making a change. Based on my research, this community was an excellent fit. I therefore agreed to meet with the Mayor and City Council in private. The Executive Search Firm handling the recruitment understood my concerns and arranged for a discrete evening meeting to be held. As I began exiting my car, I was met by the Executive Search Firm representative and quickly escorted up a private set of back stairs, into City Hall. I was seated in a room and given an opportunity to gather my thoughts before the meeting was to begin. While seated there, a woman entered the room with water and politely asked if there was anything that I needed. I smiled and thanked her for such kindness. I then asked her if everyone in the City family was as thoughtful and kind as she was? She smiled and said most were far better. We chatted for another ten minutes until the Executive Search Firm representative came into the room to retrieve and introduce me to the Mayor and Council.

A few days after this interview, I was formally offered the position. The Mayor and several of the Council members later shared with me several positive observations that caused them to unanimously offer me the position. However, one that they were all very impressed with was the glowing recommendation by their executive assistant who was kind enough to bring me water that night and sat in the room chatting with me for that brief period of time. She had shared with the Council that she thought that I was the most professional, thoughtful and caring person of all the others who had been interviewed. She also liked my shoes! She perceived me as being professional, self confident and extremely friendly. She felt very relaxed in my presence. She also mentioned to the Council that I was quite likeable and that I demonstrated a genuine interest in her based on the questions that I had asked. Without ever knowing it, the interview had begun long before I ever entered the room in which the Mayor and Council awaited my appearance! So be very aware of the first phase of the interview. You never know who may be observing or pre-interviewing you!

The second phase of the interview occurs when you walk into the interview room and are formally introduced to the Panel. Remember, as you are walking in, the panel members are instantly beginning to assess you. They are observing your looks and style of dress, your posture, gait, facial expression, and your eye contact with them individually and collectively. They are also observing your level of energy. Each of these assessments will cause them to individually begin drawing opinions about you.

Phase three begins as you are being introduced to each panelist individually. This is the time is which you want to begin initiating connections through one on one eye contact, a genuine smile, handshake and extension of brief personal thanks for their being there.

Phase four begins after you have sat down and began your opening statement. This phase allows you to set the tone for what is to occur throughout the remainder of the process. The more passionate and energetic you are in delivering your opening statement, the better you will most likely perform throughout the entire interview process.

Phase five is where you begin responding to various questions that will be posed to you. If you have properly prepared, you will most likely have identified many of the questions of interest to the panel, well in advance of the interview. This would have given you time to think through quality responses and reasons for them. Depending on the structure of the interview process, a key question within phase five may or not present itself. It is at this time when the panel will ask you if you have any questions of them before the interview concludes. You always want to have prepared quality questions to ask of the panel or hiring authority. Never, ever fail to ask at least two. Make sure that they are relevant to the panel, which may or may not be members of the organization.

The sixth phase is the closing the statement. This will normally be the shortest of all phases because in closing, you are actually summarizing your three to four major skills and strengths you opened with. This phase should only expand if you were unable to use your opening statement in the beginning. Should that have been the case, now is the time to use it as a closing statement. This phase also includes your departure and extending a thank you to the panel, the executive search firm representatives, the HR representatives and the receptionist as you depart. Make sure that you extend personal thanks to each as you depart. It only serves to boost your likability factor.

Phase seven begins when you reenter your vehicle. Take a breath, compliment yourself for a job well done and immediately begin to write out all questions that were asked. This will go into the library of potential questions you can share with your colleagues who may also be striving for the top seat. This information will also greatly assist you in preparing for the follow up interview that will be held with the hiring authority.

*"Our nation is so focused on efficiency and productivity that we forget that likability is truly our lifeline. People who are likeable, or who have what I call a high L-factor, tend to land jobs more easily, find friends more quickly, and have happier relationships."*

*Tim Sanders*

# THE LIKEABILITY OR "L" FACTOR

If you review the brochure of any recruitment effort anywhere in the world, you will find that hiring authorities list several requirements they are seeking in their next Chief. As laudable as they may appear to be, results continue to suggest that they ultimately hire for reasons not necessarily included in the brochure.

There are two reasons that appear to be most prominent. One reason is because they genuinely like you. They like you because you come across as being authentic, caring, empathic, approachable and you come across as being a good listener. It is the combination of these traits that are also referred to as the Likeability or "L" Factor. The second reason for making that hiring decision is because the hiring authority perceives you as being capable of addressing and solving issues they are experiencing. Typically, their decision to hire occurs in that particular order.

What I have observed over the many years (and this is strictly antidotal) is that most hiring entities do not want to be proven wrong in the selection of their ultimate appointee. They do not want it to be perceived as having made a mistake in judgment. So they tend to choose persons that have good solid interpersonal skills. They choose people who are likeable and genuinely friendly. This does not mean that City managers and Mayors do not want to hire the very best they can recruit. They do, but in many communities, they are under a great deal of pressure to hire based on the politics of the local community. One example of the pressure they face pertains to revenue constraints.

With difficult budgets having to be addressed year after year, most available revenue has been allocated to the public safety departments. City managers and/or mayors desperately need someone who can help par down costs. Yet, an understandable desire by public safety labor groups, who are actively involved in the political landscape, including monetary contributions to election campaigns, want a chief who cares about their members and not someone who simply makes more and more cuts. It becomes a hard task to select someone to balance these desires. This is often what drives the ultimate decision to hire someone who is likeable, which also infers credible and often a much higher priority to being technically sound. They in effect are looking for people who can work with others and jointly seek solutions. They are interested in people who genuinely listen to the concerns of others. People, who are capable of reaching viable solutions that can assist in addressing real budget challenges, while also preserving the ability of the department to respond to community emergencies.

Such hiring decisions also explain that while skill and knowledge are essential components of success, they actually account for a smaller percentage for which many will become successful. In reality, your success will be directly related to how you present yourself, your interpersonal skills, and how people perceive you. In other words, much of your success will be based on the "Likeability" Factor.

Bert Decker, a communications expert and lecturer, attributes the identification of the likeability factor to George Gallop. Gallop, a political pollster, surveyed voters to determine what influenced their decisions when voting for a political candidate. He found that there were three factors in the following order:

1) What he referred to as "the personality factor"
2) Party affiliation and,
3) Issues.

As stated by Bert Decker, the personality factor is a person's Likeability, which translates into credibility.

We need only to look back at the last several elections to determine if the likeability factor has validity. Regardless of one's political bent, Ronald Reagan was considered to be much more affable and personable than George McGovern, who came across as being less personable and stiff. Bill Clinton was much more personable and down to earth than Bob Dole. George W. Bush was more personable than Al Gore. President Obama was seen as being much more personable and likeable than John McCain. In several of these circumstances, post election surveys confirmed that people felt the candidate they selected appeared more trustworthy, credible and much more personable, causing them to vote for that particular person.

Likeability can also play a major role in whether the panelists will listen to you, believe what you are saying and value you. A 2006 NFI Research study of executives and managers across several industries found this of the study participants:

- 63% rely on a candidate's likeability when hiring and promoting
- 62% rank skills second to likeability
- 73% hire and promote based on a candidate's "ability to fit in".

Susan Guarineri, a National Certified Career Counselor and management coach, stated "the heart of likeability and approachability is about building and maintaining trust, and drawing people to you via confident and comfortable interactions."

In his book the "The Likeability Factor: How to Boost Your L-Factor", Tim Sanders defines likeability as an ability to create positive attitudes in other people through the delivery of emotional and physical benefits. He identifies four characteristics that are critical to raising ones likeability factors:

- Friendliness
- Relevancy
- Empathy
- Realness

Sanders cites numerous research studies which support his theory that, when faced with a choice among various individuals, people will choose who they like.

How do you go about increasing your likeability? Although it sounds rather synthetic, it really is not. By all accounts, likeability truly is a set of skills that can be learned and enhanced. It begins with developing a friendly mindset. Reminding yourself frequently that you are a friendly person who is genuinely concerned for others. Remind yourself that you enjoy interacting with others. Remind yourself of the positive aspects of learning from others. Don't be afraid to tell others that you truly respect and appreciate them. Practice expressing positive feelings about life and others.

Ask those around you whether or not you come across as someone who is friendly. Use their feedback as part of your critique during each of your mock interview video sessions to help assess whether or not you come across as a friendly person. Do you come across as being open? Do you appear genuinely interested in what the mock panelists or hiring authority are asking or commenting on? Is your body language congruent with your words?

People also consider you as being friendly and concerned based on your listening skills. When engaged in conversations, try listening more than you talk. Be present during the discussion. In other words, do not only half listen while you are thinking of your next response! Nod your head occasionally to let them know that they have your full attention. Instead of providing your opinion or view, ask follow up questions first. Use Rudyard Kipling's six suggested words for engaging in conversation with others. Incorporate the "What, Why, When, How, Where and Who" model to assist in showing interest in others. Be sure to follow up with clarifying questions. This simple technique will allow the other person to feel you are interested in fully understanding their comments before providing your own. Most importantly, be yourself. Show your authenticity and integrity at all times. I continually remind people I am coaching that when you are simply tolerating or patronizing others, not only do they pick up on it; they are also more apt to think less of you for it.

Likeability is crucial to the achievement of your goal to become Chief of the Department. According to a 2000 study by Yale University and the Center for Socialization and Development-Berlin, "people, unlike animals, gain success not by being aggressive, but by being nice. The research found that most successful leaders, from CEOs to PTA presidents, all treated their subordinates with respect and made genuine attempts to be liked. Their approach garnered support and led to greater success".

When's the last time you've given thought about whether you are likeable? This becomes a gut check moment. We know when we are being sincere with others. While we may state a belief in an effort to impress the panel or hiring authority, unconsciously we tend to convey our actual feelings using nonverbal behaviors during the interview. Once again I remind you, when our words and body language are in conflict, people will believe messages received from your body language. Poor treatment or lack of concern for others will also be identified during the background and reference checks. This is because a standard question asked by the executive search firm representative is how you get along with others?

Begin working on improving your "L" Factor now. It is never too late. But also understand it is a process and not a quick fix. It must be practiced daily until it becomes a part of you.

Someone once wisely stated that people would follow you anywhere if you answer through your daily actions and deeds, three essential questions:

- Can I trust you?
- Are you committed?
- Do you care about me?

So, to initiate the boosting of your "L" Factor, on a daily basis be polite, kind, concerned, open, genuine and honest with everyone you encounter. Do this by constantly displaying friendliness, relevancy, empathy and realness with others. But remember to do it with a sincere interest in mind!

*"What you do speaks so loudly that I cannot hear what you say."*

*Ralph Waldo Emerson*

# THE KEY TO EFFECTIVE COMMUNICATIONS: THE 3 V'S (VISUAL, VOCAL AND VERBAL)

I have always believed that the key to success in the public safety profession is one's ability to lead with integrity and persuade through credibility. Many have longed believed that we best achieve this outcome through effective and sincere communication. If this is true, the question we must then ask ourselves is, "what constitutes such communications and how might we improve upon our ability to carry it out?"

In 1967, Dr. Albert Mehrabian Professor Emeritus of UCLA, and two of his colleagues introduced a remarkable study on nonverbal communications referred to as the 3 V's. Although it has been a major subject of debate, it has nonetheless, greatly assisted in answering this critical question. He referred to his work as the "silent messages" in an effort to demonstrate how people communicate implicitly their emotions and attitudes. The debate exists primarily between psychologists, communications consultants and trainers. Many psychologists have cringed for decades about how communication consultants and others have misleadingly cited the results of this study when working with their clients or providing public presentations. At the center of the debate is a formula that resulted from the study. Based on the study, the researchers allocated values representing the importance of how a message is communicated. They concluded the following:

- Your body language or the visual aspect—55%
- Your tone or the vocal aspect—38%
- Your words or the verbal aspect—7%

In effect, based on the Mehrabian study, they found that 55% of communicated information that is taken in by the listener is due to visual aspects such as how we look, our gestures and other body movements. 38% is from the vocal aspect, meaning our tone and inflection, and only 7% is due to the verbal aspect or content. The formula findings came from two studies that were conducted. They asked participants to judge the feelings of a speaker by listening to a recording of a single word that was spoken in different tones of voice. The first study rated the feelings of the speaker after listening to each of nine different words. The words spoken were often inconsistent with the tone of voice used. For example, the word "brute" was spoken in a positive tone. The participants rated this single word each of the nine times they were asked to listen to it.

The second study used only one word as well. It was chosen to be as neutral as possible. The word chosen was "maybe". Again, the participants listened to a recording of the word "maybe" which was spoken in different tones. Each time the word was spoken, the subjects were shown photos of different facial expressions. As a result of these two studies, the formula was born. Today, the debate continues as to whether or not people have misused the findings in its application and therefore have questioned the actual value of each of the three V's. Some argue that to focus on the visual and vocal while ignoring the words is completely misleading. Many opine that words have significant value and play a tremendous role in establishing credibility and persuasiveness equal to that of visual and vocal.

Because each study used only one word by which to develop its findings, I would agree that the formula is most likely not applicable when applying it to interviews, speeches and comprehensive conversations between people. In fact, I would venture to say that based on comments attributed to the researchers themselves, Dr. Mehrabian and his colleagues would probably agree with this as well.

While the study may have limitations, it nonetheless brings new meaning to the words of Ralph Waldo Emerson, who once stated, "What you do speaks so loudly that I cannot hear what you say". This becomes a rather poignant statement when considering what the study actually does reveal. When our words and non-verbal messages are in conflict, listeners will believe the non-verbal aspect every time. If they do not see you, such as during a telephone interview, the listener becomes much more affected by the quality of voice as opposed to the words themselves.

Clearly, all three elements are essential to effective communications. Therefore, as you prepare for your interview, throw out the formula. Instead, always keep in mind that the three V's are the manner in which we each express and interpret messages.

When applying these findings to the interview process, once again they remind us that people will immediately begin their assessment the minute they see you walking through the door. They are determining for themselves whether or not you look and act like that of a fire chief or chief of police. They will have begun making this determination before you begin to speak. So let's discuss the importance of each element regardless of the assigned percentages.

**Visual Impact**
Through years of observations during interview processes, I have learned first-hand that people remember more based on what they see and feel as opposed to what they hear. When you enter the interviewing room, the panels' first impression of you will be based on your appearance. Subconsciously, they will decide how they feel about you based on whether or not you are dressed appropriately, appear professional, and look like a leader. Immediately following this mental assessment, other visual elements will be included in this analysis.

They will probably ask themselves the following questions:

- Beginning with posture, is the candidate standing erect and with confidence?
- Has the candidate made eye contact with us? In other words, has the candidate acknowledged my presence?

- Does he or she appear pleasant?
- Does the candidate smile or appear nervous or intense?
- Do their body gestures comport with that of a leader?
- Are their body movement's open or closed suggesting they are being protective?

Each panel member will go through this subconscious analysis. Your appearance, posture, eye contact, facial expressions, body gestures and movements will influence them each as they establish for themselves your perceived level of professionalism. The assigned level of professionalism will then expand to your credibility, likeability and trustworthiness. All of this will occur in a matter of seconds. It underscores the importance of the first V, the Visual.

**Vocal Impact**

The manner in which we speak also impacts our ability to effectively communicate. Once you begin speaking, your tone, volume, speed, pitch, diction and intonation will all play heavily into whether or not people will choose to continue listening to you. They may hear you, but listening and hearing are separate and distinct functions in communications. I may hear a low or extremely loud sound in the distance, but have absolutely no understanding of its meaning or purpose. To avoid such an unwanted outcome, be aware of your speech patterns. During your practice sessions and review of your videotape, pay careful attention to the speed in which you are speaking. For most people, our speed of speech tends to increase when we become nervous or excited. Also be aware of any tendency you may have to speak in a soft or monotone voice. This will cause the panel to have to work too hard to understand and pay attention to you. Do not be afraid to place emphases on words of importance when making a point. Always use descriptive, simple language when communicating with the panel. If you are not sure of how to pronounce a word or are not sure of it's meaning, do not use it. Use short sentences, but be sure to make your point. Never use industry jargon and buzz words! Lastly, to be impactful with your words, work to eliminate use of fillers or colloquial terms in your communications. To the extent possible, fillers such as 'er, um, uh, you know' or 'it's like", should be eliminated. With continuous practice and a goal to eliminate their use, it is quite achievable.

Ultimately, you want to pretend that you are sitting with a very close friend or family member that you respect and admire, but who you are very comfortable with and trust completely. In such settings, you are typically relaxed, personable, genuine and open. This level of comfort and openness is exactly what you want to project to the panel.

Remember, effective leaders must be able to clearly communicate to others and take responsibility for ensuring that their message is clear, concise, persuasive and impactful. We do this best with our clarity of thought, enthusiasm, energy and passion that we incorporate into our chosen verbiage.

## Verbal Impact

The verbal of the three V's should never be underestimated. Words are extremely important. I explained at the beginning of this book the objectives for having written it. I want to again caution that this book is not intended to be a short cut in your efforts to achieve your rank of choice. It is not for the shallow or lazy. I assume that you have invested the proper time and attention to studying your industry, investing the necessary time to stay abreast of trends and then, with proper word choice, articulate the state of your profession and where you plan on taking it, in a clear and concise manner. How you say something is very important, but having something of substance to say is equally important. Unless you are speaking to a panel of public safety experts, as stated previously, avoid the typical industry buzzwords. Use common English to explain your points of view.

There is an old Texan phrase, "All Hat and No Cattle" which refers to someone with style and no substance. Style as we know is very impressive and it can initially be given high marks by the panelists. But it means absolutely nothing if you do not combine it with substance! Trust me, without substance; it becomes a matter of time before it is apparent to the panel that you really do not have a full understanding of the issues. It is a killer moment in the interview process and most panel members will begin to tune out at that point anxiously waiting to get through the interview because they have already failed you.

Articulation of a complete understanding of your profession, and its future possibilities, combined with the challenges and opportunities in the department and the community you are hoping to lead, are so very essential to one's leadership ability and ultimate success. It is not only important to be able to correctly articulate problematic issues, but what you have done to improve them in your current position as well. This is one very important clue for panelist. If you can discuss what needs to be done to change an organization or resolve a problem, but cannot demonstrate what you have done or attempted to do in your current assignment to implement such strategies, it comes across as "All hat and no cattle" in living color! When discussing your views, make sure you also discuss how you have implemented them and what benefit was derived from this effort.

To have a successful interview, you have to not only know what you are going to say, but to also know how you are going to say it. This means ensuring that the three V's are fully incorporated into your preparation. Do not assign any one of the three V's less importance than the other two. In the interview setting, I consider each of them to be valuable and each one helps the two others to strengthen your presence with the Panel.

In my opinion, each of the three V's must be in perfect harmony with one another. Your ultimate goal is to have your words, tone and body language be congruent with one another. Their synchronization will only come about through daily practice and weekly review and critique of your videoed sessions.

Remember, we get one opportunity to make a good impression! When properly taken advantage of, it will successfully demonstrate your self-confidence, and establish your professionalism, credibility and trustworthiness. All are the leadership qualities important to the panel and the hiring authority.

## The Telephone Interview
As a way to confirm their interest in each of the candidates, the Executive Search Firm may choose to conduct an initial interview by phone. Such initial interviews will be scheduled in advance and it therefore gives you ample time to prepare. You will want to gather copies of all

the information you sent to them and have it in front of you during the discussion. This is to ensure consistency if you are asked about such things as dates of previous employment, promotions or assignments. You will also want to have your strategic plan and playbook handy. In addition to using it as a reference in responding to their questions, take this opportunity to also inquire about information you may need as well. This would include issues the city or department is facing or the city's current and projected financial position. It's an opportunity to ask about the level of moral and any specific concerns of department employees. You can ask for any insight regarding the city manager or mayor you will be reporting to and what their true desires are in filling this position. You can then include this additional information as part of your data collection.

Immediately following the completion of the telephone interview, it is equally important for you record in writing each of the questions you were asked and your answers during the discussion. Many times, the types of questions asked can serve as a preview for the interview process. Remember, the Executive Search Firm has already gathered information about the city's needs, having spoken to the hiring authority about the qualities their preferred candidate should possess and has an understanding of the issues confronting the organization.

Whenever we speak to someone for the first time by phone, we create an image of the person based on his or her voice pattern, energy and word choice. Prior to the scheduled phone interview, practice increasing the quality of your voice. If you are a soft-spoken person, practice increasing your volume. If you are a bit monotone, practice modulating your voice. If you speak slowly, practice increasing your speed and rhythm. Remember the 3 V's. Because you will not be seen, the vocal portion of the 3 V's now become even more important. Throughout the interview, make sure that you demonstrate enthusiasm and a sincere interest in the position. You do not want to come across as being unsure about your interest in the position. If you are one of the people the hiring authority is considering eliminating because they only want to interview a set number of persons, you want the Executive Search firm representative to argue for advancing you because of your sincere interest in the position.

*"The body never lies"*

*Martha Graham*

# UNDERSTANDING BODY LANGUAGE (YOURS NOT THEIRS)

**M**uch has been written about the art of reading the body language of others. Several books have been written on the subject, but one of the true vanguards of this art includes Nierenberg, who wrote, "How to Read a Person Like a Book". It remains available in paperback today should you wish to read it.

Learning to properly interpret the meanings of one's body gestures can be a valuable tool. But in the interview process, I have always recommended against it. Experts in this field will tell you that to properly interpret someone's behavior, you need to first have a baseline of the subject's habits and behaviors to measure against. They will also tell you that to properly read body language, it require observing clusters of signals and postures, all of which depends on the subjects mental and emotional state at that particular time. Clusters are believed to be far more reliable than attempting to read individual elements. This is not to say that some behaviors are not rather obvious, but many gestures in and of themselves can have several possible meanings.

It is for this reason that I encourage people to manage those areas they truly have control over. In other words, you are better off managing your behaviors and gestures. By taking this approach, you can focus your attention on minimizing the possibility of the panel misreading your body language. Remember one of the key findings of the Mehrabian study was that a great deal of communication results from non-verbal communication. When we are unsure about what was said, we believe the non-verbal message.

In this chapter I will attempt to address those areas that will have the greatest positive impacts to your interview.

## Posture

Within the first 5 seconds of entering the interview room and before you have uttered one word, the panel will have begun mentally accessing and passing judgment on you. Research shows that as you enter the room, your posture, body gestures, and gait will tell the panel you are either confident or not. Our body language is the most powerful way of communicating our confidence than anything we may say. Before you reach them, most will have formulated an opinion in their mind as to whether or not they feel you are the right person for this position. This will be based primarily on whether or not you appear confident. Do you represent a good fit for their community? Do you appear credible? Are you a leader? All of these questions will be partially answered based on how confident they perceive you to be as you enter the room. This is the very reason for the saying, "You never get a second chance to make a good first impression!" It is also very important to understand this initial assessment will positively or negatively set the tone for what is to follow. There is nothing harder than trying to claw your way back after receiving a poor first impression! Given their initial mental assessment, they will spend the remainder of the interview seeking information that confirms their view. This is why you never want to initially place yourself in a poor position.

If you look at any past or current leaders throughout this world, they each have at least one very important thing in common. They each stand erect with incredible upper body posture. Our posture is considered a reflection of our beliefs about who we are and what we are capable of. It reflects the confidence we have in ourselves. People with poor upper body posture are often perceived as persons who feel inferior due to low self-esteem. It is certainly one reason for which you will always see world leaders making sure that their posture reflects one of strength and confidence. After all, if they do not appear to believe it, why should others?

To improve upon your posture and increase your sense of confidence, I found a valuable exercise said to be used by models, actresses, actors, and some world leaders. It has been referred to in many ways. It was introduced to me as the "Four point Posture improvement Technique." Use of this exercise causes you to first begin experiencing the feeling of proper upper body posture and then you will gradually become accustomed to walking in this manner on a regular bases through change of habit.

**Four Point Improvement Techniques for Posture**
Begin by standing up against a flat wall with both feet together. Press the heels of your feet directly against the wall. Now press your buttock and the small of your back onto the wall. Once you have accomplished this, press your shoulders onto the wall. Although it will initially feel strange, stand there for two to three minutes and consciously make yourself aware of every aspect of this new feeling. Now, take two steps forward and release any tension in your body. Gently shake yourself to loosen any feelings of stiffness. Now, walk away from the wall maintaining the same erect posture. Releasing any tension allows you to avoid walking robotically. You want to be relaxed. Use your arms and hands as you normally would but make sure that they are not creating closed positions. Walk around while maintaining this posture. Do you feel the difference? Can you feel a greater sense of confidence in yourself as you gracefully walk around?

Do this exercise as often as possible each day and you will be surprised at how natural it will begin to feel and how different you will begin feeling. You will acquire a greater sense of confidence and before long; others around you will begin sensing it as well. Include a warm genuine smile with your practice as well. When you walk through that door to the meet the interview panel, they too will instantly notice the confidence. It will also translate into the look of a Leader!

**Eye Contact**
Have you ever heard the phrase, "The eyes are the window to our soul?" Well, many experts believe it to be true. The eyes can send many different non-verbal signals. Looking into the eyes of the person we are speaking to is a normal part of how we communicate. Many of us have

acquired the basic ability to interpret messages conveyed by one's eyes. Through the observations of one's eyes, we have learned to determine the feelings of others, including comfort and discomfort, at a very young age. Our eyes can readily reveal such emotions as excitement, concern, fear and trouble. What is not spoken out loud can in fact be expressed through the eyes. Some basic points about our eyes:

Research shows that when we are nervous our blink rate tends to increase. While experts acknowledge that it can be the result of stress, they also acknowledge that it can be associated with being dishonest, which is what most untrained people immediately equate it to. Another misconception involves that of little or no eye contact. Many perceive such behavior as a classic sign of deception. Someone who begins looking away during the interview while being asked a difficult question will most likely leave the panelist with the belief that they are intentionally avoiding the question. If you fail to make eye contact when answering a question, it will most likely to be perceived as a lie. Research however, suggests just the opposite. People who are being deceptive know you will be looking at their eyes so they make a point of looking directly at you to throw you off. However, because laypersons associate this behavior with lying, always maintain reasonably eye contact when responding.

What is also important to understand is how we behave in certain stressful situations? Knowing how we typically respond allows us to decide which behaviors to change so that we avoid having others draw false conclusions. For some, making eye contact can create nervousness in and of itself. However, when we make eye contact others feel good as it shows your level of interest in them. If you are one who gets nervous when making eye contact, practice focusing your attention on their nose. They cannot tell that this is where your eyes are focused and will assume you are looking them in the eye. Just make sure that you do not get so comfortable with your stare that you suddenly make them feel uncomfortable because you never pan to the other panelist.

Eye contact is also very important for persuasion. To effectively persuade someone in the interview process or attempt to change their mind if things did not start out so well, you will want to first gain good eye contact with them and then sustain it with regular reconnections as you pan the panel. During the interview, when responding to a question, you will want to spend approximately forty percent of your eye contact with the person who asked it. The remaining sixty percent should be equally distributed between the remaining panel members. This will allow all members to feel included in the conversation.

## Facial Expressions

Our face is another area of the body that reflects our mood and feelings of the moment. It provides the viewer the ability to detect levels of comfort or fear. Many people are not aware of their facial expressions when entering the room. But it is an essential area of the body that must be managed if you are to achieve desired results. Your goal is to enter the interview with a genuine, warm smile on your face. According to researchers, when we smile at someone, it stimulates a bundle of neurons in the frontal lobe of the receiver's brain, triggering happy feelings. In other words, by simply delivering a pleasant, genuine smile while entering the interview room and especially while introductions are underway, it could subconsciously start to associate elation with you. The combination of your posture reflecting confidence and a genuine smile begins to establish that personal connection with each individual panelist, before you begin the interview.

## Open versus closed body positioning

We present ourselves in various manners and a great deal of it is due to our comfort of habit. Avoid creating closed body positions when entering the room and while seated with the panel or hiring authority. This would include the folding of arms across your chest, hands in pockets, crossing of legs or feet. It also includes your body turned slightly away from others.

## Being Attentive

When you are attentive to what each panelist are saying, it is perceived by the recipients as being extremely flattering. Appearing attentive is extremely important in a one on one setting with the hiring authority. It also causes the recipient to want to provide you with the same level of courtesy. Showing real interest in what other people are saying creates connections and feelings of support for one another. There are several ways in which you can demonstrate such interests. They include:

## A Tilted Head

A person who is attentive will tilt his or her head slightly forward. When tilting to the side, it can be perceived as being curious or uncertain.

## Leaning Forward

This is another body language gesture associated with reflecting an interest in what the other person is saying. It also allows you to better hear the other person.

## Open Body Positioning

Shows you are mentally open to what they have to say and not the least bit defensive.

## Gaze

Attentive persons maintain their gaze for slightly longer periods and typically will blink less for fear of missing something.

## Slow Nod

A slow nod, especially when combined with a slight forward lean and head tilt, encourages the person to continue their comment or question. It also indicates your understanding and approval.

## Patience

We are much more patient when we are interested in hearing more of what they are saying. Being patient means not interrupting the person who is speaking, even if they briefly pause. Be especially observant of methodical type persons who tend to carefully pose their questions in a systematic way. Allow them to complete their comments before beginning your response.

*"People will forget what you said
People will forget what you did
But people will never forget how
you made them feel".*

*Maya Angelou*

# Establishing an Instantaneous Bond

Your ability to connect with the panel will directly influence how you are ultimately rated. As you can well imagine, it is much easier to create connections when you and the panel share similarities in some obvious way. But how do you create instant bonds with people who are different than you, whether in ethnicity, gender, nationality, life style choice, age or ideology? Today, most progressive cities make every effort to ensure that the panel is balanced or at minimum, reflective of the community. But depending on where in the country you are applying for that top seat, this may be a challenge, thereby making it even more important for you to establish an emotional bond.

The opportunity to create a bond or connect with your panel begins the moment you walk into the interview room. The recommended techniques that I offer are intentionally designed to be subtle to avoid your coming across as being disingenuous or manipulative. When the techniques are combined, they will leave the panel member with a positive experience. Many times, they will not be consciously aware of what caused the connection to have occurred, but emotionally they will be left with a positive feeling, which is precisely what you want.

When first entering the interview room, enter with good posture and briefly scan the room with a pleasant smile. This will make you look more positive to your panel. Immediately engage in eye-to-eye contact, initially with as many panel members as you can, then one on one as you move towards each person while being formally introduced. When being introduced, many candidates tend to look through, around or away from the person as they are being introduced. Others without realizing it will briefly look at the individual they are being introduced to, but will then unintentionally turn their attention to the next person to be introduced to causing the one you are still standing in front of to feel slighted.

To avoid this, as you turn to each person, focus your full attention on them as though they are the only person in the room. Make cheerful "eye to eye" contact. This simple act sends a subconscious message to the person that they matter to you.

Take a few seconds with each panel member as they are introducing themselves to you. Use such techniques as repeating their name, thanking them for there presence, telling them how privileged you are to be there or what a pleasure it is to meet them. This creates intimacy and friendship.

Extend and maintain a "genuine" and warm smile. Smiling indicates happiness and a friendly attitude. As stated earlier, smiles cause a chemical release in our brain that also causes a similar type of response from the receivers of the smile. To gain the benefit of the chemical release, the smile has to be genuine. It's important to also understand that people can detect a fake smile. A genuine smile involves the whole face and includes the eyes. If it will help, prior to the day of the interview and then prior to walking into the room, have an incident or favorite memory in mind that has caused you to smile. Think of it while walking into the room. Remember, a genuine smile includes the eyes as well so make sure that the past incident or memory is one that invokes a special moment that caused you to beam.

Another powerful, yet subtle technique is to practice the art of providing an equal amount of pressure that is applied by each panelist during the handshake. People have a tendency to bond or connect with those they feel are like them. This simple technique provides the other person with proof that the two of you are very much alike. As you near the panel member, angle your extended arm and hand across your chest, with your thumb up. Lock hands, thumb joint to thumb joint.

Then, allow the person to initiate pressure first. Immediately after they began applying pressure, begin matching it so it is equal to theirs. Stop applying the pressure as soon as they stop. Pump a minimum of two but no more than three times and then initiate release. Those with a gentler handshake will appreciate that you both share the same style of grasp. Those with a firm grip will also appreciate someone who has a firm grip as well. Focus on matching grip pressure and always avoid making assumptions. I have found that men tend to be more biased when it comes to shaking hands with women. They will either falsely assume that it will be a gentle clasp or if their style is to apply a firm grip, they do so without regard for the impact to the woman. Using this technique allows anyone, man or woman to not apply biases and instead, appear similar to one another.

If you are a person who tends to have clammy palms in these settings, fear not. While approaching the first panel member, allow your right arm and hand to casually drop down to your side as you enter the room or as you approach the person. Using a very subtle move, lightly brush the palm of your hand against your pants or skirt drying it as you raise it to the handshake position. To perfect this move, practice it during your taped video sessions to ensure that it is undetected.

An additional technique during the interview itself would be to subtly mimic or mirror the interviewers body language and to speak with the same speed as that of the panel. This is extremely effective during a one on one interview. Also, carefully listen to word choices that they each use and then incorporate them in your responses to them. Their word choices will also tell you a little about the way in which the person processes information. The continual use of such words as "I see" preceding their sentences could suggest that they are more visual. This will require you to be more descriptive. Regular use of the phrase, "I feel" can suggest they are emotionally driven, so demonstrating sensitivity in your presentation would be useful. Continuous use of the phrase "I think" may suggest thoughtful, methodical reasoning. Expressing yourself in the same manner, with the same use of words choices and rhythm, could be very beneficial. This is especially true in a one on one setting.

*"I had luck and tenacity. And, yes . . . . the appearance that can make it a little easier."*

*Paul Newman*

# LOOKS DO MATTER

Studies have determined that looks do indeed matter when people are making decisions about you. Panels tend to value ones attributes, just as much as a person's intellect. The combination of both can make one quite formidable. Do you look like a Chief? Do you look and act energetic? Are you personable? Are you pleasant? Are you engaging? Are you physically fit? Do you have striking features? Clearly, not all of us are as fortunate.

Unless we are willing to subject ourselves to cosmetic surgery, we cannot change our God given features. However, the good news is that we can do several things to improve upon our appearance and enhance the way we are perceived by others. One particular way is to improve upon our fitness. By improving upon our fitness we began feeling better about ourselves. When we feel good about ourselves, we project a greater level of self-esteem, also making us appear more attractive. Feeling better about ourselves also improves upon our performance in interview settings and life in general. Why? Because when you feel good about yourself, your confidence level significantly increases. The improvements will be both physical and psychological. Regularly exercising improves on our vitality, energy, physique and self-esteem. Another way of enhancing our appearance is with our style of clothing. A genuine smile on our face also enhances ones appearance. Exhibiting exuberance, confidence and passion can also improve on how we are viewed, as well and these are all elements within our control. However, our physical appearance will be the focus of this chapter, as it will provide a multitude of benefits.

**Benefits of Exercise**
If we isolate the value of exercise to just the interview process experience, it provides tremendous benefit. Exercising weeks in advance of the interview will give you an incredible edge psychologically and an improved visual appearance. We feel better about ourselves because we suddenly began feeling and looking better. These benefits alone will give you an incredible edge going into any interview environment. But, there is another valuable benefit as well. It also gives you increased energy which is also important to reflect during your interview. Remember, the receptionist, panel members or hiring authority will begin accessing you within the first five seconds of meeting you. They will be mentally determining whether or not you appear confident and look like their next Chief of Department. Remember also our discussion about the three V's? Visual is extremely important to people when determining how they feel about a person.

In addition to improving on your appearance, exercise also helps to protect your health. As a future Chief of Department, you will be in stressful situations as it relate to various responsibilities. Situations such as numerous public appearances, difficult budget sessions, and major emergency responses can each have an impact on you. By investing in your health, you will be insulating yourself from the negative health effects that these stressful situations could ultimately have on your body. New research has also shown that regular exercise can make you smarter, snappier and even mentally sound. Exercise has been shown to actually enhance the development of new brain cells in the region linked to age-related memory decline that begins around age 30 for most people. All are great benefits to have as part of your arsenal as you pursue your goal. If I have not already convinced you of the importance of either continuing or immediately beginning an exercise regimen, here are two more benefits.

**Exercise = More Energy and Makes you Happier**
Studies consistently show that physical activity increases mental alertness and energy, while reducing fatigue. Mounting evidence proves

that exercise is as good for your mind as it is for your body, thanks to elevated levels of feel-good chemicals like endorphins. And as we have discussed, happier people are much more exuberant and people pick up on it immediately. This will greatly benefit you in the interview. Happier people also typically smile more often than others who are less happy and doing so can actually cause others to have those enduring feelings about you.

## Implementing An Exercise Regimen

With a great degree of hope, I am going to assume that you are already involved in a regular exercise regimen? If not, now is the time to get serious about your health and welfare. Needless to say, the stress and demands of a leadership position, which are high, are reason enough. Our body's ability to endure the many stressors depends on how well we manage stressors in our lives. One sure way to manage stress is through regular exercise.

If you are not currently involved in an exercise program, before jumping into anything aggressive, make sure you first visit your doctor. Until then, begin by simply walking a few miles each day. The key is to not allow procrastination to prevail. Start now and slowly build up. Each day you should engage in some form of exercise. Create an exercise sheet section in your playbook. Set goals for what it is you are wishing to accomplish. Log your daily activity. Review it weekly to give yourself encouragement and to track your progress. If you have difficulty staying on track, you may consider engaging the help of a personal trainer. This will not only allow you to remain motivated (because you are spending money for it), but it will also keep you on track through a well-designed program. Most gyms provide this option, but make sure you discuss your goals with the trainer before deciding on a particular program. Be specific as to your desired outcome regarding weight loss, toning or increased energy. Other options include the use of DVD programs. There are several on the market, but avoid being too aggressive if you have been sedentary. This option allows you to work out in the comfort of your home at your own pace and preferred time of day. Again, be sure to track your progress by logging in the type of training you engaged in daily and the amount of time invested.

If you are interested in losing weight, a program that has positive short and long term effects for individuals is the Weight Watchers program. Not only is it reasonably priced and very effective, it also gives you the option of participating in person or on line. The program is designed to change poor eating habits as opposed to dieting, which is why it has such a high success rate. Regardless of what program you choose, you want benefits that are long lasting, physically and mentally.

Whether it is exercising to improve your vitality, energy, physique or self-esteem; style of clothing to enhance our overall appearance; a genuine smile or walking through that door exhibiting exuberance, confidence and passion—you can enhance your appearance by improving on several elements within our control.

Remember, your ultimate goal for engaging in this effort will be to have your body and mind as well tuned as possible.

*"I am the Greatest"*

*Mohammed Ali*

# THE POWER OF DAILY AFFIRMATIONS

Research has proven that incorporating the use of daily affirmations becomes a highly recommended powerful tool that greatly assists you in achieving your goal. Affirmations have been used by some of the world's highest achievers to aid in positively programming their subconscious mind.

An affirmation is a statement of declaration. It serves as a reinforcing technique to manifest, strengthen or program a desired belief or outcome. The daily use of positive affirmations can serve as a highly effective attitude adjustment technique as well. Despite the amount of documented research in this area, very few individuals have understood or appreciated the positive impact that affirmations have on ones psyche. Nor have they recognized that as one improves upon their attitude and self worth, it has an incredibly positive impact on others around them.

If we were even partially aware of the many benefits of positive affirmations, we would immediately cease the negative self-talk we tend to routinely engage in. I am not referring to the occasional self-effacing we may engage in from time to time as a way to show that we do not take ourselves too seriously. In these situations, it is appropriate to demonstrate that we can laugh at ourselves due to a particular situation. But many people, on a daily bases, tend to engage in self inflicted character assassinations against themselves without realizing just how damaging it is to their self worth and attitude.

After experiencing a negative situation, how many times have we said to ourselves, "I knew that was going to happen"? How many times have you scolded yourself making such statements as, "you idiot" or "damn it, you dummy, what were you thinking?" Many engage in such negative behavior from time to time, but it is important to understand that it is not what the successful tend to do.

Successful people understand the importance of being selective with their thoughts. They purposely insulate themselves from self-inflicted attacks on their character and self worth, intuitively understanding that negative self-talk also gets programmed into our subconscious. This does not mean that they foolishly mislead themselves. We all make mistakes and gaffs from time to time. However, instead of using negative self-talk, successful people have learned to state it in an entirely different manner so that they program the correct message into their subconscious mind. Instead of saying, "damn it, you dummy", they tell themselves, "this is not like me, I am better than this, next time, I will do better!" This is an entirely different type of messaging. It allows us to acknowledge our error without tearing ourselves down.

For affirmations to be effective, they must be formatted in a specific manner. First, they should always be stated in a first person format. When developing yours, use only the first person pronoun "I". Second, they should always be stated in the present tense. "I am". You then follow these two words with the desired results you seek. As an example, "I am a Fire Chief"! "I am the next Police Chief for the City of . . . . "!

Equally important to the success of this technique is to state each affirmation with conviction, passion and enthusiasm. Begin now to develop affirmations to manifest your career desires and any special traits important to your journey. Once you develop them, write them out and include them as part of your playbook. Most importantly, immediately begin affirming them as often as possible. Do so upon awaking each morning. As a new ritual, start affirming them out loud while in the shower, while getting ready for work in the morning. Affirm them while driving to and from work. Affirm them just before falling asleep. Remember to affirm them with all the conviction, passion and enthusiasm that you can muster!

You will be amazed and excited by the gradual change you and others begin to see in your attitude and demeanor as your subconscious mind begins moving you towards the desired traits and outcomes you seek. People will begin seeing you as the passionate, enthusiastic Chief of Department in waiting! They will know the next Chief of the Department has just entered the room!

A word of caution while engaged in this daily exercise. Make sure that you state these affirmations out loud and with conviction and enthusiasm. But, make sure you are out of public sight. You do not want people thinking you are starting to lose it!

*"Clear The Mechanism"*

*Billy Chapel*

# "CLEAR THE MECHANISM"

In the movie, "For the Love of the Game", Kevin Costner portrayed a veteran pitcher named Billy Chapel for the Detroit Tigers. Chapel had reached the pinnacle of his career when he suffered a horrific injury to his pitching hand. He worked to get back to the field even though others questioned whether or not he could successfully return to his prior level of play. He returns and a few years later, with a 19-year career behind him, he had to now make a second decision about whether or not he was capable of extending an illustrious career just a little longer. Like so many of us in actual life, he was faced with the difficult decision of calling it quits. I will not destroy the movie for you by explaining how it ends and will instead allow you the opportunity to see it. But, during the end of the movie, you will find some of baseball's best strategies being presented!

The most fascinating scenes in the movie occurred each time Billy Chapel took the mound. Amidst all the different sounds of a ballpark, including the obnoxious boos and taunts of the opposing teams fans, the various yells and comments, food vendors hawking their products throughout each section of the park, the never ending ballpark music and announcements, he employs a unique technique. A technique that is important for us all to employ from time to time.

As any baseball fan knows, a pitcher must have absolute concentration on the mound and therefore must be able to block out such distractions, not obsess on the last pitch, the last hit, or the last poorly thrown ball in the dirt, but instead remain in the moment and focus their attention on the catcher. To achieve this, Billy Chapel had developed a way of literally drowning out all the distractions. He would put himself into the moment and block everything else out. He achieved this state of mind by saying to himself, "Clear the Mechanism!" Then all at once the ballpark noise and distractions vanished. He was now completely in the moment, focused only on his catcher and the placement of his next pitch.

Invoking key words designed to signal to your brain to get into the moment is imperative. It allows you to properly prepare and ready yourself mentally. It allows you to focus solely on the matters of importance when beginning your practice exercises. The purpose is to get into the right state of mind allowing you to learn and retain. Why is it important to incorporate this technique into your daily practice? It is important because we all tend to multi task far too often in today's society. While it is great to be able to do so in certain circumstances, it is not in this case. It is crucial that you set everything aside and clear your mind. It is important to let go of issues you must follow up on after spending time preparing for your interview. It is important to clearly define in your mind's eye specifically what you're wishing to accomplish in this practice session.

Clear the mechanism and concentrate on the objectives you have set for each practice session. Whether it is to clearly see every aspect of the interview in vivid detail while using all five of your senses as you perform perfectly in your interview, or to focus on the elimination of the use of non-words, maintain control of your body language, show energy, or increasing your likeability factor, you must first get into the moment. Whatever the purpose, clear your conscious mind of distractions, declare and then focus on the desired outcomes so that your subconscious mind and nervous system can imprint within only what you are wanting to accomplish!

Below are some strategies you can use to mentally clear your mind and prepare it to receive the input you desire to be imprinted.

**Focus on the moment**. Too many times we are so busy thinking of issues we need to address that it causes us to be somewhat distracted.

This is especially true if we are aware of a problem awaiting our attention or an issue that did not get resolved to our liking. Remind yourself that during this time of practice you will focus only improvement. The last matter or the impending one will be there after you have finished. Give yourself permission to set them down for an hour or so with the understanding that you will return to them immediately following your uninterrupted practice time.

**Begin each session in the same way.** Always begin by first reading the Vision and Goal statements in your Personal Strategic plan. Then read each of the reasons you have outlined that explains why this so very important to you. This simple effort will provide you with purpose and a reason to focus.

**Commit to not begin the practice session until you have cleared your mind.** The worst thing we can do to ourselves is to think we can proceed even though we are still mentally multi-tasking. You will have wasted the time and energy so seek full commitment before beginning. If you feel you are losing your focus, stop and remind yourself what it is you are attempting to achieve.

**Seek the support of your spouse or significant other.**
Ask family members to screen calls or keep the kids busy while you take the necessary time to prepare in a quiet place. Unless it is an emergency, getting back to others within an hour or two is not unreasonable.

Remember, "Clear the Mechanism" (or whichever choice of words you decide to use), is a reminder to eliminate all distractions and substitute them with objectives you want to focus on. With this strategy you will maximize on the benefit of the practice session. More importantly, you will also eliminate the guilty feelings we tend to engage in when we can't be in two places at one time.

If you have never seen the movie, go and pick it up. It's a keeper!

*"Always be a first rate version of yourself instead of a second rate version of somebody else".*

*Judy Garland*

# Your Opening and Closing Statements

You have now completed your self-assessment and have identified those special skills and strengths that you possess. These attributes also serve as the underpinning for your personal brand. It is now time to develop that opening statement to the panel and hiring the authority. A well crafted statement that highlights the unique skills and strengths that only you can provide to the organization.

In the vast majority of interviews, you will be invited to provide an opening statement regarding your background and experience. Typically, they will begin the interview by asking you to begin by briefly telling them a little about yourself. This is considered your opening statement. The opening statement is so critical to the establishment of the right tone in your interview that I have chosen to address it separately. It should never be less than two minutes and never longer than three. Most candidates will walk into an interview setting, get settled in, and when asked to say a little about themselves, will begin to provide a chronology about their life. This is not what you want to share with them. Remember such a chronology is in your the resume that is most likely at their place setting. Given your time is limited and your goal is to demonstrate why you are the right choice, it is important to maximize on every second of time.

The purpose of an opening statement is three fold: it is the opportunity to share with the panel your three or four very well thought out skills or strengths that are uniquely you, setting you apart from most others. It is the opportunity for you to relate these attributes to the position you are seeking to fill, demonstrating the great fit between you and the position. It is an opportunity to establish the right tone for the remainder of the interview.

Your opening statement should be designed in such a way that it purposefully pulls the panel into those areas you want them to follow up on with you. An example of such an opening would go as follows:

Lead Panelist: Why don't we begin by having you briefly tell us a little about yourself?

Candidate: Let me begin by once again thanking each of you for the opportunity to be here this morning. I am excited about the possibility of joining such a warm, inviting community and a stellar department. I recognize that you have my resume before you. However, in addition to the listed experience and educational achievements on my resume, I would also like to briefly discuss the three major skills and strength's that I have successfully developed during my career. These unique attributes, in my opinion, would serve as complimentary skills to the City and they would greatly assist me in leading the department while achieving its short and long-range goals.

First of all, I have developed great interpersonal skills. I have the ability to work with and through individuals at all levels of the department, throughout the city structure and the community. With the use of this skill, I am also able to successfully lead the organization toward the achievement of the critical goals and objectives that have been outlined for this community.

Second, I have developed excellent conceptual skills. I am able to provide guidance and assistance to my staff on multiple projects while maintaining an overall focus on the broader vision for the City. Through the use of these two skills, I am able to explain to the workforce the importance of what and why they are assigned to specific tasks each day and how they fit into the larger picture regarding the City's stated goal.

Lastly, I have great diagnostic skills. I have the ability to take large complex problems and break them down, layer by layer, until I am able to identify the core issue. From there, I am able to craft real solutions that not only address each of the layers of concern, but of equal importance, I am able to design solutions that prevent the organization from ever having to redress the core problem again.

It is the combination of these three attributes and the tremendous amount of success I have been able to achieve with them; the experience that I have acquired through the various assignments and responsibilities throughout my career, and the formal education that includes a Bachelors and Masters degree in Public Policy that gives me the confidence to immediately step into this position. I consider my skills and the requirements of this position as an excellent fit. With my sincere hope of earning your support this morning, I would be honored to apply each of these attributes and all of my experiences to the betterment of this organization and community.

What have we done here? First, we have provided them with an opening that had a maximum duration of two to three minutes. We have stated just enough to get them intrigued without having them worry about time management. Second, we have introduced special skills and attributes that are uniquely you without boring them by simply regurgitating information in your resume, which is before them. However, you highlighted portions important to the position. We are prepared to give them actual examples of where each of these skills has been successfully utilized. But for now we have created an opening designed to draw them back into a discussion with you on those things you are most comfortable in explaining. We have also asked for their support in this endeavor. Lastly, we have made it clear that we are not exploring. We are interested in this position.

## Closing Statement

The closing statement is given at the end of your interview. When the panel has completed asking you the prepared set of questions, they will generally end by saying "We have completed the interview, is there anything you would like to conclude with?" If you have performed well, you will want to provide a very short summary.

Always begin by thanking the panel for the opportunity to appear before them. Let them know that you considered it an honor to participate. Summarize your three (or four) strengths by stating something like, "I would like to conclude by stating that I feel privileged to be here this morning. I truly believe that my three unique skills will greatly benefit the department and City. They include my interpersonal skills, which allows me the ability to work well with others, my conceptual skills that allow me the ability to manage multiple department projects while always maintaining a focus on the City's overall vision and lastly my diagnostic skills, which provides me with the ability to carefully analyze and identify the core problem and then apply the best solutions regardless of how complex the issue. Each will serve as great assets and I am committed to utilizing them to the betterment of the organization and community. I would consider it an honor to join and lead this department. Thank you once again."

Then immediately begin standing so that they know you are done. They will begin to rise as well. Extend individual handshakes using the same technique as previously described. Maintain a warm smile and good eye contact with each as you shake hands. After leaving the room, be sure to thank everyone you come in contact with that was a part of the process.

Never introduce anything new at this point. Stay on message re-enforcing your primary strengths.

The only time you would close with anything longer is if you were not able to provide an opening statement. At the beginning of some interviews, the panel may go right to the first question and not ask that you provide them with an overview of your past. In this instance, you will want to close with the originally prepared opening statement.

*"The only person that can keep you from achieving your dreams stands before you in the mirror each and every day!"*

*Dorothy Gwendolyn Ewell*

# Incorporating Stories and Quotes

Throughout my childhood, my voracious reading Mom would always recite quotes to motivate and inspire us. Little did we know the vast majority of quotes were often altered? As we grew older, and she forced us to read more, she eventually had to confess that she took the liberty of changing many of the quotes as a way to re-enforce her message. They each served as an important part of our early "education in life" and we each carry them with us today.

There was seldom a day that went by without my Mom reciting at least one. You could count on her inserting one or more when explaining to us that our homework did not reflect our best effort or if we were not presentable enough as we prepared to leave home for the day. If we came home complaining about how difficult a school assignment was she would quickly respond by saying "Nothing is impossible if we hold on to our faith"! When my siblings and I were not dressed according to the standards she had established in our home, she would remind us "Clothes do in fact make the person (man)". If any of us would dare complain about someone else attempting to make our life miserable or trying to hold us back, we could always correctly anticipate her response; " The only person that can keep you from your achieving your dreams stands before you in the mirror each and every day!"

Such quotes cultivated our attitudes and taught us the importance of resolve as we grew up. Their daily reminder convinced us that if we maintained faith in God and ourselves, nothing could keep us from achieving our goals. We were taught to never allow others to decide how far in life we were to go and to take full responsibility for our choices.

Later in life, as I began interviewing for positions, or providing direction to my staff, I found myself incorporating her words of "altered wisdom" into my own comments.

Several years ago, while interviewing for a metropolitan fire chiefs position, each candidate had to rotate between three different panels. One of the three panels was composed of prominent members of the community. It included three women and two men. Three introduced themselves as educators. One educator was from a nearby university, one from the community college and the other from the school district. A question posed to me by the professor at the nearby University, was management related. "How do you remain relevant and stay abreast of changes in management principles?", she asked. I had prepared for the possibility of such a question because during my research, I found that the community considered the department to be a traditional based organization. I intentionally paused for a second and then offered a slight smile. I smiled because I suddenly heard the voice of my Mom. In response to the question, I included two of her quotes.

I explained that I was raised with several axioms that formed my belief system. Two in particular have served to motivate me to always strive to remain relevant and stay abreast of the latest management principles. My Mom instilled them both in me. The first principle she taught us is that "Ignorance is not bliss, nor will it ever be!" and the second is that "What you don't know will hurt you!" These teachings have motivated me to always strive to maintain awareness and understanding in four key areas that have allowed me to remain relevant by keeping abreast of essential matters important to my career.

The first area is that of the Fire Service industry itself. I have always been fascinated by the history of the fire service. How it originated, how it was and is now funded, and how it has evolved over the many decades. I stay abreast of worldwide trends that seem to emerge on a daily basis. I read industry related studies about the direction of the

Fire Service and alternative funding available to municipalities. I use this information to brainstorm with my staff, the many possibilities we should contemplate pursuing in the interest of the community I currently represent. In addition, because of limited resources we are each experiencing at the local level, we brainstorm about ways we can combine activities to reduce cost while also improving on services essential to residents.

The second area of study is the national economy. I recognize that being a Fire Chief is more than simply managing the women and men of the department. I have a duty to assist the City Manager in anticipating funding challenges due to a struggling economy. Staying abreast of the national economy allows me to anticipate and properly plan for either the receiving of federal resources to carry out our mission or a possible reduction due to a weak economy. I believe it to be a failure of my management ability if I were to simply wait until we loose our funding before seeking alternative ways to provide services to our residents.

The third area is national politics. I stay abreast of national politics, not because I am being political, but because it to helps me in understanding where the country is heading. Based on political views and who is in the majority, it allows me to be prepared for policy shifts that can directly affect my ability to deliver essential services locally.

The last area is the study of people. It keeps me focused on how to lead, manage and motivate those around me and those who report directly to me. The panel responded quite favorably.

I was offered and accepted the position. Approximately one year later, I saw the Professor at a reception. She said to me, "I knew that you were the right person for the position. Not only were you professional, you were also quite personable and well grounded. Anyone who is comfortable enough to cite teachings from their Mom and acknowledge the vital role she played in ensuring you dedicated your life to continuous learning, is not only well rounded, but quite grounded in my view". I walked away from the professor saying to myself, "Thank you so very much Mom!"

Over the years I have continued to test out this theory of incorporating quotes and stories as a way to demonstrate realness. I find that people greatly appreciate short, appropriate quotes or stories as a way to underscore or reinforce a critical point you wish to make. Depending on the chosen story or quote, I have found that it will also signal to the panel that you possess broad interests and are open to applying solutions to issues that originated from outside your profession.

One of my favorite observations occurred while serving as a panelist for a Police Chief selection process in a major city. The candidate was asked a "what if" question regarding a disciplinary problem within the department. This question was purposely included by HR because the department had been rife with personnel problems throughout the past several years and the rank and file were completely fed up with what they perceived as a heavy handed, disciplinarian style of management. The candidate responded by stating that while he firmly believes in administering discipline commensurate with the infraction, he also believed in people. He asked us if we would please indulge him while he shared a brief story with us that would assist in explaining his management philosophy? We each nodded in support of his doing so (an excellent technique used to capture the panels undivided attention). He paused momentarily and then proceeded to share with us a fable written by Aesop:

> *"The Sun and Wind were in an argument as to who was the most powerful. The Wind said, "I will prove I am the stronger!" Do you see that old man down there? I bet that I can make him take off his coat quicker than you can. The Sun agreed and slipped behind the clouds to observe the Winds efforts. The Wind began blowing with all his might. He blew so hard that he nearly caused a tornado. But, the harder he blew, the tighter the old man wrapped his coat around himself. Exhausted, the Wind gave up. The Sun then came from behind the clouds and began smiling kindly upon the old man. Pleasantly, the old man wiped his brow and pulled off his coat. The Sun then turned to the Wind and said that gentleness, warmth and friendliness are always stronger than fury and force"!*

He went on to explain that Aesop was said to be a small, deformed man born into slavery in the 6$^{th}$ century. Yet he knew more about how to work with people and to persuade them to do what was needed, than anyone of his time and maybe even ours. While it may have a short-term effect, most people automatically react unfavorably to force, threats, intimidation and demands. In my experience, leading with friendliness and professionalism begets the same in return.

The candidate concluded by stating that he believed his style of management was even more important today than ever before. "We have what is referred to as the Gen Y generation entering the Public Safety profession today. They are not as tied to jobs as we may have been when we began our careers. A top down management style does not inspire them. They are heavily involved in social networking, which means that they text, tweet, email and blog with one another daily to keep up to date on what the best managed departments are doing to encourage inclusiveness. They are heavy users of new technologies—they can take current technology and actually manipulate it to expand its functions beyond its original design. They use this skill to enhance their ability to carry out their work on and off the job.

Most importantly, they want to be included in establishing a positive direction for the organization. They have far fewer social issues than past generations. They grew up in multicultural environments with different ethnicities, genders and alternative lifestyles and are quite comfortable with this new norm. They understand the need for maintaining a paramilitary structure in the public safety sector. But where and when it makes sense, they expect open dialog and inclusiveness so that they can feel valued and are able to contribute. With this new reality in mind, I have found working with people, listening to them and their ideas while exhibiting consistency, kindness and fairness in the workplace, just as Aesop had suggested centuries ago is still a far better approach."

He had done his homework, was aware of the department's history and the undertone that existed within the organization. After utilizing this story, he said to us that he took his responsibility as head of the department quite seriously when it pertained to addressing violations. When appropriate, he can be firm. But whenever possible, his goal is to correct or eliminate the problem while developing the individual. He was hired, enjoyed a successful career and became known as the best Chief of Police that community had ever experienced.

When identifying stories and quotes to incorporate into your responses, remember that there are rules that must always be adhered to:

- The story or quote has to be short and to the point. If it is too complicated or long, you will lose the interest of the panel.
- It must be germane to the topic.
- Never use anything that can be viewed as political in nature, even if you think you know where they stand politically.
- Use only gender-neutral stories or quotes.
- Never use them more than once in any interview setting (so have several in mind that can relate to potential questions that you have will most likely come up)
- Never ever use "off color" material.
- When using borrowed stories or quotes, cite the appropriate source. Not only is it professional to do so, but you also get extra points for citing reading materials outside your industry. Both will reflect well on you.
- Never use this technique to emphasize negativity. Use it only to reinforce a positive point.
- Above all, make sure that the selected stories or quotes are offered with sincerity as to how "you" truly feel or believe. People can detect insincerity a mile away!

In utilizing this technique, people will view you as someone who is real and authentic. They will see you as someone who is friendly, personable, warm and down to earth! Such attributes are valuable to have as a Chief of the Department in any community!

*"I wish I had an answer to that because I'm tired of answering that question."*

*Yogi Berra*

# FIVE LIKELY QUESTIONS TO ANTICIPATE AND SUGGESTED WAYS TO RESPOND

During the interview, there will be several different types of questions you will need to be prepared for. There are open-ended questions that allow you to take the answer into any direction that you choose. These types of questions allow the panel to gain a better understanding of your logic. There are closed end questions that are designed to simply get a straightforward understanding of your position on an issue. They are least utilized in the interview process but they can come up. There are also situational questions designed to get you to explain what you would do in a particular set of circumstances? This type of question is designed to understand your thought processing ability. There are also behavioral questions used more and more often today to get an understanding of how you have behaved or responded in the past to particular situations. The theory behind this type of question being, given how you responded in the past, it can serve as a predictor to how you will most likely respond in the future. Regardless of the question, it is imperative that you avoid canned answers.

All responses must be offered with sincerity, passion and authentically. To achieve this, you must speak from personal experience or researched knowledge. These two approaches are what allow you to appear real to the interviewers.

By tracking the local newspaper in your city of interest and by engaging in the collection of data found in the Vision Based Strategic Plan and Playbook, you will get a greater sense of the potential types of questions to anticipate. In perusing the local newspapers, look also for crime blogs and any consistent complaints found in letters to the editor as a way to better understand concerns of the community. Another approach is to call the local Chamber of Commerce. Let them know that you have an interest in applying for a position with the City and wanted to gain insight from them as to the issues they believe are of greatest concern. You may also want to check with local neighborhood associations as well. They will provide an entirely different perspective and will appreciate your outreach and interest from their perspective. If you have already applied for the open position, prior to making any of these contacts, be sure that the Executive Search Firm or Human Resource Director handling the recruitment is comfortable with you making such inquiries.

In larger cities, one issue that continues to be of paramount concern is that of gang activity. Across the United States, part one crime continues to be in decline. Conversely, throughout most of the nation, gang activity has steadily increased. This is an area that both a Police Chief and Fire Chief candidate should be prepared for. As a Police Chief candidate, it is quite obvious as to why you should be prepared to discuss national and local trends, as well as strategies that appear to be working in other areas. As an example, through the use of algorithms, the trend now appears to be "predictive responses" as a way to allocate resources and get ahead of the problem before it occurs. In many States, police departments are partnering with the district attorney's office and are filing lawsuits against individual gang members. Many departments are heavily involved with Federal Task Forces so that they take advantage of federal charges, which will put the bad guy away longer and typically remove him or her away from the local community.

The point is to have a well thought out strategy you can discuss with the panel and be prepared to share how it is working elsewhere. If it is a new untried approach, such as the recently enacted laws in such states as Arizona, allowing you to determine one's legal status in the course of a pre-text stop, be prepared to discuss the fact that you have vetted it to ensure it meets with any legal concerns, including complaints of targeting any particular ethnicity group. Finally, be prepared to discuss how you would introduce it or any other new strategy used elsewhere, to the community. Keep community buy-in foremost in your mind. Telling the panel that you would meet with the community in advance of implementation, discuss current crime stats and explain why and how this new strategy will be beneficial to the neighborhoods being inundated with crime, is essential. It will go a long way!!!!

As a Fire Chief candidate, even if you were not asked this type of question, if gang violence is rising, you should be willing to state to the panel as part of your discussion that you are quite aware of the level of gang violence in parts of the community. You can explain that you bring this matter up for a host of reasons. First of all, your members will be responding to gunshot victims and will also be responding in areas where gang violence and errant bullets have no regard for the life of others whether they are firefighters, EMS personnel or the general public. You should also use it as an opportunity to share your belief in partnering with the police department and community to do your part to assist in curtailing or eliminating gang violence. Whether it is to have your staff serve as the eyes and ears for the community when they are out on inspection, during emergency responses or when assigning staff to schools, you want them to know that you intend on being part of a long-term solution that benefits all residents. The point in doing so would be to show you are a team player who is focused on the needs of the community and City as a whole.

Whatever the reasons you may choose to use, I can assure you it will reflect well on you. All communities appreciate people who are concerned about the total well being of their neighborhood.

Your goal in responding to any question should always be to:

- Re-enforce your credibility
- Demonstrate leadership qualities.
- Demonstrate your communication skills.
- Demonstrate your passion, enthusiasm and energy.

Remember also, panels respond favorably to candidates who exhibit a sense of fairness, balance, character, strength, interpersonal skills, and a desire for getting things done. But above all, they want a leader who has an affinity for their community.

In addition to the most likely questions that you determine to most likely be asked based on your data review, there are five basic questions that you should always be prepared to respond to. If they are not asked, you should be prepared to incorporate them in your responses to other questions.

**Question 1**: Briefly tell us about yourself?

The primary purpose for this question is to allow the candidate to relax and settle into the interview. It's traditionally been referred to as an icebreaker. However, the more astute candidates should be prepared to maximize on this opportunity. For a full explanation, go to the chapter on your Opening and Closing Statement. Your response should be designed to reflect your unique, specialized skills and abilities that only you are capable of providing. In doing your homework, to the extent possible, your attributes should align with the needs of the organization and help to address problems the department is currently experiencing. This will help to demonstrate that you are a value added asset.

**Sample response**: Refer to chapter 19, Your Opening and Closing Statements.

**Question 2**: What was the greatest challenge you have had to face in your current assignment, what was the outcome, and how did you resolve it?

This is a question that allows them to predict how you will most likely respond to a challenging situation in the future. Answer with honesty. In this situation, it becomes an excellent opportunity to disclose a challenge in your past by sharing it with them before you are asked about it. If such an issue exists in your past, now is the time to disclose it so that you can demonstrate what you learned from the experience and how it has made you an even better leader today.

**Sample Response**: "I was given a vote of no confidence by the Union members in my last place of employment. The unions' reason for which this vote was taken was because I refused to yield to what I considered to be an inappropriate operational change. The Mayor, Council and City Manager all supported my reasoning. Although I felt confident in my position, in retrospect, I could have handled it differently. I did not have to be so rigid and I could have used this difference of professional opinion as an opportunity to open, not shut down dialog.

Additionally, I now realize that this was the time to be more visible throughout the workplace. This would have allowed me the opportunity to discuss my reticence for the proposed change based on my applied logic. By not being more visible, it allowed others to express my professional views based on their perspective. This was not the wisest decision I could have made. While I cannot always assure you that this type of action will never occur again, I can assure you of one very important thing, that I will not allow it to fester simply because I stood on principle and therefore refused to further discuss it with the union leadership and most importantly the members of the organization".

**Question 3**: What do you consider to be your greatest weaknesses?

They are interested in knowing just how honest you are and how well you know yourself. Experts suggest that you attempt to state a weakness that is really a positive in disguise.

**Sample response**: "I am a person who tends to focus my attention on the bigger picture when dealing with issues within the organization and city. Because of this, at times, I may miss some detail as a result. To ensure that I not miss details critical to the best interest of the organization, I have learned to assign someone who is detailed oriented to assist me as I work through the issues. This has served me in two important ways. 1) I do not miss important detail. 2) I have now become much more sensitive to the importance detail and I am now identifying it 95% of the time. I continue to improve upon that remaining 5%.

**Question 4:** If you were directed by the City Manager or Mayor to make reductions to your department budget that you felt would compromise public safety, how would you handle the request?

For many, this is a difficult position to be placed in, yet panelists are asking this type of question more and more often. Once again, answer with honesty.

**Sample response:** I would ask to meet with the City Manager or Mayor to discuss the implications of the reductions. I would make every effort to convince them to reconsider based on my professional concerns. I would also ask for time to seek alternative solutions that would get them to their desired reduction goal without compromising public safety. However, the bottom line is this, I work for him or her. I am a member of their executive team. We are one city. Therefore, if I could not convince them to change their thinking, I would ask that when I present my proposed budget reductions publicly, that I be allowed the professional courtesy of preferencing my remarks by first stating that I fully understand the financial dilemma we currently face and the need for reductions to be made citywide. However, such cuts are not without negative implications. I would then state the potential negative impacts based on my professional experience. Under no circumstances would I ever attempt to dramatize, overstate or incorporate the use of scare tactics.

**Question 5:** Do you have any questions?

This is a question that all candidates must be prepared to respond to. Never say" I do not have any questions at this time" or that "you answered all my questions during our discussion". In 101 Dynamic Questions to Ask at Your Job Interview, Richard Fein, placement director at the University of Massachusetts (Amherst) School of Management, reported that more than half of 1,000 employers surveyed nationwide said that the single most important reason to ask this question is because the candidates questions are a means of evaluating your fitness for the position. From your questions, Mr. Fein explains, employers can determine how seriously you about the position and how well you understand the nature of its duties.

With this in mind, never ask "me first" questions that benefit you. Such questions would include your starting salary or the entities vacation policies. Ask questions that make you appear genuinely interested and well prepared for the position.

**Sample response**: I enjoy working interdepartmentally to assist in addressing citywide issues of importance. Does the senior team work well together?

**If you are interviewing with the Hiring Authority another example could include:** I was impressed with your Mission and Vision statement in the budget document. How do you hold your Executive Team members accountable for ensuring we are working to achieve them?

Prepare at least three such questions that you can ask the panel and three you can ask the hiring authority. You may not get to ask them all, but always attempt to ask at least two appropriate questions such as those above to demonstrate your interest in the position and the fact that you have done your homework.

*"Everyone visualizes. Losers visualize the penalties of failure. Winners visualize the rewards of success."*

**Dr. Rob Gilbert**

# MENTAL REHEARSAL OF VISUALIZATION

Visualization is the practice of running through various scenarios in your mind prior to them occurring. This technique allows you to become mentally experienced in an event before it has ever taken place. Mental rehearsal of visualization first became popular in the Soviet Union. Scientist began using this technique as a way to prepare Soviets in areas such as education, sports and science advancement. Many decades' later, countless individuals from virtually every industry known to mankind employ this proven technique as a way to prepare themselves for key events.

A leading expert in this area of study is Dr. Charles Garfield. He holds PhD's in both Mathematics and Psychology, and has studied this area of science for years. He is considered one of the foremost authorities on the subject peak performance.

This technique requires the engagement of all five of our senses while using vivid, detailed mental images as you go through the entire desired performance you are seeking to achieve, over and over again in your mind. It requires that you first get into a relaxed state of mind so that your subconscious mind can etch into memory each detail. Because the subconscious mind and central nervous system cannot discern reality from make believe, we are training our mind and body to perform in a specific manner, especially when under pressure. Brain studies have confirmed that thoughts produce the same mental instructions, as do actions. Because the subconscious mind now assumes that it has done this act several times before, we are able to become more relaxed and go through the desired motions during the actual interview process because we have vividly watched ourselves go through it countless times before in our minds eye.

Research has also documented that when we combine mental rehearsals with actual physical practice, the outcomes are even more effective than using either alone.

It has also been proven that mental imagery has a positive impact on several cognitive processes in our brain. It improves upon our motor control, our perception, planning and memory. This technique has also been found to increase one's confidence and enhance our motivation. All of these byproducts are extremely beneficial to you as you prepare and participate in an interview process!

The great golfer Arnold Palmer allegedly once stated that he has never addressed a ball without first seeing it in his mind's eye and experiencing the shot exactly as he expects it to have occurred. Virtually every high performing person in literally every professional industry will tell you they engage in this very same technique. Whether it is a special board meeting, a big presentation or speech, most business professionals and athletes prepare by engaging in this technique. This is exactly the way you must begin preparing for your interview session well in advance of the day it is scheduled. See it in your mind's eye. See it in vivid detail and color.

I must again state that it is imperative that you incorporate all five senses during each of your mental rehearsals. The more vivid it is, the more powerful the results. Remember, our subconscious mind and central nervous system cannot distinguish a visualized vivid thought as not having actually occurred yet. The more you mentally rehearse with perfection in mind, when you do go into the actual interview these two systems assume that you have actually done this several times before. Therefore, the signal they send to your conscious mind and body is "there is nothing to get overly stressed or worried about"! Let's go in and enjoy this experience again! Let's do it as perfectly as we have each and every other time!

Begin now to include this technique in your preparation efforts. Use it daily. I always encourage those I am working with to begin each morning prior to getting out of bed, by engaging in this powerful exercise. And each evening prior to falling asleep, do the very same thing.

In a vivid, detailed manner, see yourself dressed in a professional well-appointed business suit. You are well groomed from head to toe. As you exit your car and walk toward the building where the interview will take place, see yourself being relaxed, standing tall and walking with a sense of confidence and humility. See yourself entering into the waiting area of the office and cheerfully greeting the receptionist with a smile and introducing yourself. As you are lead into the interview room, see yourself walking in with shoulders squared, standing erect and relaxed. You have a warm smile and possess that sense of confidence. You are excited and enthusiastic about the opportunity to discuss your qualifications, your values, views on management and above all, the opportunity to be considered for the top position in this particular community. As you're being introduced to each of the panelists, see yourself extending your dry hand out to shake hands with each of them. See yourself making and maintaining 'eye to eye' contact and that it is accompanied by a warm genuine smile as you greet them individually. See yourself exhibiting a warm appreciation for the opportunity to meet them as though they were friends from your past. Feel the energy in the room. Observe how impressed they are with you. See yourself standing next to the chair you will occupy momentarily but not being seated until they have asked you to do so. Now, physically adjust the chair so that when you are seated, the panel can see you from the waist up. See them asking you to begin by you briefly sharing your background and qualifications with them. Hear yourself as you deliver that well prepared opening statement with poise, energy and perfection. Have you included all five senses in this mental imagery exercise? Have you included all the detail you can?

Each day, as you engage in this technique, you will begin noticing an increased sense of confidence starting to develop as you incorporate every detail of the interview from start to finish. Make this a part of your daily routine.

*Lights, Cameras, Action!*

*D.W. Griffith*

# VIDEOTAPING AND CRITIQUES

U sing the NFL as an example, during and after every game, people are assigned the critical responsibility of carefully reviewing every inch of videotape taken during the game. They look at each and every motion of every player. They carefully review each response to each move and overall play. They are looking for positives results and any flaws in their game strategy. They are also seeking ways in which they can take advantage of situations being played out on the field. As they study this film, they seek to make appropriate adjustments and refinements that will make them more effective.

This is precisely the type of critique that you must be willing to make in reviewing your interview practices. Having a congruent message verbally and non-verbally are key to your appearing sincere and credible during the interview process. It is the reason for which you must identify and address any nervous movements or bad habits that you may unknowingly engage in, especially while involved in the interview. Bad habits, such as a nervous laugh, fiddling with objects on the table, clutching or rubbing your hands or wiggling your fingers for example, are all habits that many engage in during interviews. Most, including seasoned interviewees, do not even realize that they are doing it. Yet, when you combine such movements with a statement like, "I am very confident in my abilities as a leader" or, "I am very patient when dealing with my subordinates"—you will not be believed.

For these reasons, it is imperative that we learn more about our own habits and work to correct them prior to the interview and for the remainder of your career. Keep in mind, as Chief of the Department, your workforce and the community will also notice and pass judgment on these incongruence's as well.

The good news is that we can correct bad habits. Habits as you know are learned. We can therefore unlearn them. We each have at least one bad or nervous habit that we revert back to during moments of stress. Some time ago, subordinates made me aware of my own habit. I was initially in denial about it. After it was brought to my attention, I began paying more attention to the associated patterns of my behavior. Sure enough, whenever someone or something would annoy me, I would engage in a particular habit. Today, I have successfully been able to eliminate that particular pattern of behavior that was so noticeable to everyone but me. This does not mean that I no longer have any other habits or nervous patterns. Truth is, after retiring, I stopped being concerned about any remaining ones. However, when we are aware of those that we possess which are incongruent with our words, we should take advantage of the opportunity to address them.

The two best ways of identifying any annoying behaviors we have are by first asking people closest to us for brutally honest feedback. The second way is to review and critically critique your video practices. Begin by discussing with individuals' closes to you your desire to try and eliminate any annoying or perceived nervous behaviors that you have acquired over time. Let them know in order for you to grow, you need their honest feedback in identifying them. Let me say that few ever make such a request because we tend to shy away from hearing anything that is less than flattering about ourselves. If you fall into this group, you are robbing yourself of an opportunity to better you!

Listen carefully to their feedback with sincere interest. Do not challenge them when they are providing you with examples. Ask them to clarify their observations if necessary. Ask them if there are times in which they notice these annoying behaviors or habits more often? This allows you to better isolate the behavior pattern. Lean slightly forward towards them while discussing their concerns with them. Maintain good eye contact and nod with agreement if they are pointing out gestures that you are aware of, but have never attempted to correct in the past. Ask if there are other behaviors you should know about and thank them for their willingness to share this information with you.

Recognize that in addition to getting valuable feedback on what habits or patterns you need to change, you are also practicing on improving your listening skills and enhancing your "L" factor!

Ask multiple persons so that you get a more accurate list. Now take that list and set it aside. Next, at your earliest began videotaping your rehearsals. During the first practice session, be yourself. Now, review the video with the list of suggested concerns others have shared with you. Begin identifying the shared concerns and any others that you have noticed. Also, make sure that you review each taped practice session with a goal of improving on your techniques. Be critical. Have your family members and close confidants review it with you. Allow them to offer their feedback and consider it objectively. Understand that most people dislike looking at themselves on tape. They focus on silly things that are not important. "I am losing my hair" or "look at how grey I have gotten" some will say. Focus on the critique list items that I have included below.

During your mock interview sessions make sure that you include at least one full dress rehearsal as part of your practices. This will allow you to make any adjustments to clothing selections. Try and make these fun sessions. If you have family or close friends, let them play the role of the panel. Provide them with potential questions and ask that they randomly select a few to ask of you. Enjoy the exercise while you improve.

## Critique Check List of Video Observations

- Posture and facial expressions while walking into the reception area.
- Posture and facial expression as you enter the interview room. Are you being robotic or are you relaxed and flowing gracefully?
- Did you thank the receptionist or person who escorted you into the interview room?

- Extending your arm to shake hands with good eye contact and a pleasant/ enthusiastic smile. Don't forget to also practice the clammy palm maneuver.
- While taking a seat, have you properly adjusted the chair to ensure you are viewed from the waist up from their vantage point? Physically moving the chair will also keep you from inadvertently encroaching on their table space. It also allows you to utilize your hands and arms (using open gestures) without banging the table.
- Is your opening statement, complete, inspirational and heartfelt?
- Are you using non-words and fillers?
- Are you responding directly to the questions asked and then explaining reasons for your answer?
- Are you staying on message and not offering very long answers?
- Are you scratching your face or touching parts of your face as you speak?
- Are you fiddling with your glasses?
- Are you adjusting portions of your clothing?
- Are you perspiring?
- Pronunciation of words (remember the 3 V's)
- Are you leaning slightly forward while making key or important points?
- If you are using your hands while expressing yourself, which is considered a good thing, are they being used with open gestures?
- Are your legs or feet crossed?
- Are you maintaining pleasant facial expressions?
- Are you maintaining good eye contact (40% for the person asking the question and the remaining time shared equally between the others)
- Are you enjoying yourself?
- If it is a dressed rehearsal, is your selected clothing enhancing your appearance?
- Is your Closing Statement, well summarized, given with energy and poise? Did you rise from your seat first?

*"The Best revenge is Massive Success!"*

*Frank Sinatra*

# FRANK SINATRA AND YOU!

Regardless of how ambitious or defined your goals are, regardless of how positive your attitude or the number of affirmations you state each day, regardless of your planning and sacrifices made to achieve your dreams, there are always going to be people around you that for one reason or another, will attempt to tear you down. People, for whatever reason, will be envious of you, your goals, your discipline and especially the vision that you have for your life. I have a long held belief that the more ambitious and successful you become, the more you will attract and encounter these negative and insecure individuals! Who knows why some will attempt to dissuade you or try and tear down you and your dreams?

But understand it is not important to know why. Look at it for what it is—one of the many mysteries of life we must accept as a shortcoming in human beings. Throughout your career, you will readily recognize them. They are the small-minded who prefer to band together because they do much better in groups as mal-discontents. They will level virtually every negative comment conceivable at you, especially behind your back. You will hear comments such as:

- "He was hand-picked and did not deserve it."
- "She only got the job because she is a woman."
- "He has no real experience".
- "She was quite cozy with the politicians".

When these days come, and trust me they shall, you will have a wide spectrum of responses to choose from. One end of the spectrum will include those who choose to seek revenge and on the opposite end of the spectrum there will be those who will wisely choose to extend forgiveness.

In deciding where you land in this spectrum of choices, should revenge become important to you, let it be the type of revenge offered by Frank Sinatra. When being criticized by both friends and detractors, he reportedly reminded himself "The best revenge is massive success!" At minimum, this option keeps you from wallowing in the very muck and behaving like those you find yourself upset or disappointed with. Quite honestly, your ultimate goal should always be to stay out of the muck. Given Sinatra's level of professional success, in the end he certainly was able to silence his critics. More importantly, he silenced them without ever having to retaliate against them or lower himself to their level.

The quality that has historically separated great men and women from the little people in life is the degree to which we ourselves participate in such narrow mindedness. Always keep in mind that how you handle the criticism that is destined to come your way will directly reflect upon the level of confidence and self worth you possess. The world is replete with examples of leaders who chose to focus on their goals and not react to such pettiness. It is a choice we each have.

Abraham Lincoln was famous for looking beyond the criticisms and vicious attacks made against him by others. In fact, he was so well schooled in understanding the importance of not seeking revenge and the valuable energy you lose as a result of engaging in it that he appointed many of his detractors to his cabinet. Despite the fact that Seward, Chase and Stanton each openly criticized the President, referring to him as a clown and guerilla, he nonetheless appointed them each to his cabinet.

One of the oldest documents known to mankind, the Bible, is also replete with examples of people who understood the importance of ignoring one's critics, choosing instead to overlook unconstructed criticism and remain focused on your goal.

Take a moment to read the Parable of the Sower. It too teaches us the importance of staying focused, as he wisely remained in the field and kept sowing seeds despite the fact that the birds of life, the weeds, and the many cares of life all descended on the seeds in an effort to disrupt the sowers goal. He clearly understood the importance of staying focused on his vision and not his detractors.

It simply is of no value to debate or attempt to get even with others who choose to disagree with you or who try to keep you from your dreams. It is their prerogative, and attempting to get even with them will be of more harm to you than it is to them. It can begin to erode your self-esteem and self worth. It is important for you to always keep in mind the words written by John M. Mason, when he so eloquently stated:

> *"Revenge is like a boomerang. Although for a time it flies in the direction in which it is hurled, it takes a sudden curve, and returning, hits your own head the heaviest blow of all."*

Always remain focused on your goals and allow your successes to serve as the appropriate response, assuming you feel it is even of importance to you. To assist in minimizing the invitation for the small minded to criticize, limit the sharing of your goals to only those who have similar goals or to those who are in positions to assist you in reaching them.

The best approach in addressing such petty matters is for you to choose to extend forgiveness. Clear once and for all your own emotional state of anger and your own slate. This requires you to immediately do two things:

- Right now, at this very moment . . . forgive all those you believe to have intentionally harmed you. Those who you have secretly harbored resentment for, given their previous comments and behaviors toward you.

- Now . . . also forgive yourself for what you have said or done to others in an attempt to hurt or belittle them for whatever reason.

You are now ready to move forward without having to drag around those negative feelings. Remember, we cannot change our past actions or behaviors. We can only learn from them and in doing so, commit to never engage in the behavior again as we move forward in life. Let the small minded engage in the petty unimportant things of life. Focus only on those things that truly matter!

*"Today knowledge has power. It controls access to opportunity and advancement."*

*Peter F. Drucker*

# STAYING ABREAST OF TOPICAL ISSUES

One very important habit to get into is to stay abreast of topical issues. This should include the world economy and it's impacts to national, state and local government. It should include policy decisions that affect the thinking and mood of the country and labor issues and trends occurring worldwide. The purpose is to broaden your thinking, expand on your knowledge base and develop a more in-depth awareness on matters that directly and indirectly affect your industry.

I would strongly recommend you immediately begin reading a minimum of seven newspapers a day. You do not have to read them cover-to-cover, but look at the local section, business section, as well as the opinion and editorial pages. If you are interested in joining a smaller community, read their local paper as well and be sure to check to see if they include a crime blog that reports criminal activity on a daily bases. In review of any of the papers, identify the topical issues that are being covered locally, nationally and internationally. It will begin to give you an understanding of what is occurring throughout the world and within that community. By reading the local paper of the community you have an interest in joining, you will begin to appreciate what they consider to be most important to them. Reading a combination of the major large city newspapers and the local ones will also increases your depth of knowledge. The papers should be a mix of such daily papers as the Wall Street journal, the New York Times, Los Angeles Times, Financial Times, Washington Post, the local paper in the community of interest to you and the paper that covers the state capital for the state activities. Yes, given the change in the availability of free newspapers on line, it will cost you. But I think in the long term, the investment will benefit you. You can begin by finding out what papers your department or City Hall currently subscribe to and borrow them if you can. You may also want to check with your local library as well.

Whatever combination of newspapers you choose, make sure that you include large, median and small market area papers to peruse. The goal is to begin acquiring a broader and more in-depth understanding of key issues outside and within your industry. By reading topical events that are occurring worldwide, you will begin to deepen your understanding of the issues and it will cause you to begin thinking about possible solutions that can be applied to many complex problems. It also allows you to begin discussing issues based on a substantive and not superficial level of understanding.

As I was writing this chapter, the U.S. Senate was holding a historic vote. They voted to repeal and eliminate the "Don't ask, Don't tell" (DADT) policy of the military that prevented Gay and Lesbian personnel from acknowledging their sexual orientation preference without being discharged. This policy has been in place since President Clinton's Administration enacted it in the 1990's. During the week leading up to this vote, and the week afterwards, many of the major papers that I referenced above wrote various articles and editorials about this policy change. Most had varying perspectives. Many in which I vehemently disagreed with. However, I at least had a better appreciation for the perspective of others.

Irrespective of your personal views, have you given in-depth thought to this policy change? Have you considered how it may impact public safety? Is it a civil rights matter? Was it a discriminatory practice? Will it really affect how our women and men of uniform perform? Does the change reflect your personal values? What about the values of this country? Because this policy change has worked well in other countries, will it work here?

More importantly, how would you incorporate such a policy into your department so that it is done respectfully and not with potential animus? Given the reality that Gay and Lesbians exists, have always existed and will continue to perform in an exemplary fashion, how could you implement such a policy change so that people can freely discharge their duties without fear of reprisal? How do you set expectations within the department as to how members will comport themselves, focusing on working together as opposed to the disagreement of this cultural change? These are the very types of questions that you should be considering and developing professional positions on.

And remember, your position may or may not be agreed with, but unless it is clearly biased, grounded in hate, fear, or prejudice, most people will listen and may appreciate the thought that went into it even if they personally disagree with you. Just remember to always be willing to explain and support your reasoning with fact and logic that is backed by credible research.

What about the national healthcare debate? Have you given any thought to how this may impact (whether positively or negatively) responses to calls in the field? Does it have a relationship or impact on the reality that local governments will no longer be able to afford some health care benefits currently enjoyed by employees and retirees alike?

We will always be a country of diverse opinions and one of the goals of the interview is to understand your thinking process. What lead you to this conclusion and what facts do you have to support this view? Fully developing your own views will also spare you from being perceived as a chameleon and instead, find a community that is more closely aligned with your values and beliefs.

*"Great things are done by a series of small things brought together."*

*Vincent Van Gogh*

# PUTTING IT ALL TOGETHER

ongrats! You have now developed a comprehensive systematic plan to pursue your dream. Having assembled such a plan now places you among the elite five percent of women and men in our country who actually take the time to think through their dreams, establish a clear mission, clarify their vision and then create goals and specific objectives that will lead them to their desire. Research suggests that you are now much more likely to be successful in reaching your goal simply by having written it out. Completion of this effort also provides you with a Playbook that contains the best responses to questions that will most likely be asked during your interview. You now have methods for improvement and schedules to follow as you monitor your progress. To ensure completion, let's go through the below checklist:

| **Accomplishment** | **Check ✓** |
|---|---|
| • You have crystallized your Mission in life. | ☐ |
| • You have carefully defined your Vision. | ☐ |
| • You have identified your goal(s) and have developed objectives that will allow you to successfully achieve each goal in a specified and measurable period of time. | ☐ |

- You have established a clear set of values by which you are committed to and have prioritized them so that you can always avoid internal conflict.

- You have identified your strengths and your weakness and have began a corrective action plan to eliminate the weaknesses.

- You have included your family or significant other in the final plan review to ensure that your personal and professional goals are in alignment with one another and that they are in agreement with you given the periodic time constraints and conflicts.

- You have used all the above information to develop and/or re-enforce your Personal Brand. Also, you have ensured that your resume, CV and any other documents pertaining to you are aligned with one another. Any future articles or Blogs, even tweets and all other social networking sites, will now be congruent with your brand.

- You have adopted a positive attitude. It is one that expects the best to always come to fruition. You are also appreciative for your life and current accomplishments.

- You have developed daily affirmations that you will use several times throughout each day, which will imprint into your subconscious mind only those behaviors or goals you seek.

- You have collected key data on the community of interest to you. Based on the information you have collected, you have began identifying opportunities for change, developing potential questions that would most likely be asked and comprehensive responses that you can begin to internalize and articulate during your interview. ☐

- You have developed a strong, inspirational opening and closing statement that reflect your three to four major strengths and you are prepared to express why they are of value to that department and city. ☐

- You are consciously aware of and are practicing proper upper body posture, eye contact, handshake, smile and open body positions whenever interacting with others. ☐

- You are purposely working on enhancing your "L" Factor by the way you interact with others. Showing genuine interest in them and employing Rudyard Kipling's six suggested words. ☐

- You are consciously working to eliminate the use of non-words and fillers when speaking. ☐

- You have begun mental rehearsals, repeatedly playing out in your mind's eye, every single detail of your interview. Each time, in your mind's eye, you perform flawlessly. You are utilizing all five senses during these practices. ☐

- You have established video rehearsals and critiques. You have selected only those individuals who you trust most, knowing that they will give you unvarnished constructive feedback to ensure you are getting better with each session.

- You have begun selecting your wardrobe for the interview.

- You are not the least bit concerned by anything the naysayers may choose to say. You are focused on those things that matter.

- You have developed an exercise regimen, knowing that your health will be key not only in the performance of the interview, but also your job of choice, which is just ahead.

- You have begun expanding your friendships recognizing that in this new era, tolerance and consensus building will be key traits for the Leader you are.

- In addition to staying abreast of your industry trends, you are also reading several newspapers each day to remain abreast of worldwide, national, state and local issues.

- Prior to the interview, you have confirmed the time and have properly mapped out the location. You shall arrive 25 minutes before your scheduled appointment and check in 15 minutes before the interview.

If you have completed each of these tasks, then all that is left is for you to practice, practice, practice and critique, critique, critique in anticipation of your upcoming interview.

Now, I want you imagine you are an actor or actress who is performing tonight on Broadway. The theater is packed. They have heard a great deal about you. The lights begin to slowly dim and the curtain slowly begins to rise. It is the moment you have carefully and meticulously prepared for. Yes, you are a bit nervous, but that is only natural. You have carefully developed and rehearsed each line to perfection. You know each specific place on the stage you are to stand. You possess the incredible upper body posture and it is projecting your confidence and leadership ability. You are in command and control of your body language. Given this, you can expect to be viewed in only the best of light. Your voice is prepared to properly project the well-chosen script you have prepared. You will deliver it with enthusiasm, energy and passion. You can feel the excitement of the audience as the curtain continues to slowly rise. You are perfectly dressed. You are now prepared to deliver the type of performance that you have seen occur in your mind's eye, literally hundreds of times before. It is the type of performance that will be heralded by all as the best performance of all times. They will rave about how well prepared you were. They will marvel at how natural you appeared! How very convincing you were. How very passionate, enthusiastic and genuine you were.

They await you with bated breath. You are now ready for the curtain to fully rise!

*"It is better to give than receive—especially advice."*

*Mark Twain*

# FINAL THOUGHTS AND ADVICE

There are a few thoughts and pieces of advice that I wanted to impart, but that do not fit within the pages of the various chapters. Therefore I have chosen to offer them as final thoughts and advice.

First of all, I strongly urge you to understand the role of an Executive Search Firm and the HR department during any recruitment. They are obligated to provide the hiring authority with all pertinent information about the candidate through a thorough background review. I can tell you from having worked with several of the best throughout this country that they are very good at what they do! This is precisely why it is imperative that you always protect your reputation, live by true values, and understand that nothing is ever completely hidden or lost!

Make sure that you always maintain a solid financial history. Avoid over expenditures, late payments and heavy debt. Simply put, live within your means. Bad credit reports are red flags for any city, town or county. If you can't manage your own finances, what makes you think others will want to put you in charge of managing the publics?

Also, irrespective of how tempting it may be, avoid extra marital affairs or work related relationships. To the hiring entity, it is a clear indication of poor judgment and it could lead to potential concerns of credibility, questions of morality, and it could expose the entity to possibly future litigation if the behavior continues to persist.

Remember also that what is posted on the internet is there forever. Ask all of your family and friends to not post your photos on social network pages without you having viewed first them. Never take pictures with any alcohol in your hand or while engaged in other foolish or childish behavior. You would be surprised at how and when they seem to surface! You should also remember that the day you are declared a finalist, every person with a computer and internet access will begin to Google your name. Do not give them reasons to come before City Council raising concerns about the person that is being considered. You can't eliminate a bad article, but you can control it. Apply the strategies found in the chapter "Establishing your Personal Brand." Let the articles and blogs you engage in about activities pertaining to your industry be what they find most often.

---

Regardless of your political views or party affiliation, during your climb I strongly urge you not to contribute to individuals running for local office, especially in Mayor, County Executive or Council elections. As you know, anyone can check the campaign contribution rolls and find out who the donors were. If you supported the candidate who lost and not the one who won, it could be problematic. Conversely, if you supported a candidate who won and not the one who lost and then the loser ran again in the next election cycle and won, well I can only tell you they probably will not have forgotten. Besides, you never want people to assume you were appointed or were able to keep your position simply because of your campaign contributions. It can also make it difficult to establish credibility with your workforce. It may suggest to some that you are political as opposed to being a professional. It creates a no-win situation and any good politician knows it places you in a compromised position. If they have ethics, they will understand your reluctance. I recognize that you have a right to participate in these elections and I encourage you to always cast your vote in the voting booth. But contributions are not worth the controversy that may follow. If you feel you really want to contribute, do so through a surrogate.

---

Let me re-emphasize another critical point. Throughout this process and your career, it is imperative that you be yourself. Live your values. It is the only way that authenticity and the "L" factor will shine through. Remember, throughout this country there are literally thousands of communities who will welcome persons who are liberal in their thinking and there are thousands who will welcome those who are conservative in their view. There are also thousands of communities who will gladly welcome either. So never feel you have to change who you are during the interview in order to get the job. And always remember, the one thing that every community wants is someone who is professional, honest and committed to the welfare of their residents.

---

Over the past decade, the nation and world has become more and more divisive. Much of this divide appears to be along ideological lines. Another contributing factor has been a weak economy. During such periods of near or actual recessions, we tend to experience a greater level of animus between ethnicities and economic strata. Because we live in a multi-cultural society, tomorrow's leaders must find ways to motivate, persuade and lead all, period. To avoid becoming overly insular, provincial and uncomfortable around people who are not like you in whatever manner, begin now to expand upon your circle of friendships. If you are a Democrat, find and create friendships with those who are Independent or Republican. If you are a Republican or Independent, begin expanding your circle of friends to include those with different views. If you are Black or Hispanic, expand your friendships to include all other ethnicities. If you are White or Asian, begin expanding your circle of friends to include all other ethnicities as well. Always be willing to place yourself in new situations. Gain comfort and the necessary skill sets to create relationships despite differences. It will enhance your ability to work with, through and lead all personnel. This is in complete contrast to what many engage in today, which is to avoid those that are not like them. The only requirement in expanding this circle of friends is to only choose those who have dreams and goals of their own and who possess a generally positive attitude.

---

If ever given a choice, always choose to be either the second person interviewed that day or the last. As second, you get the benefit of the panel establishing a rhythm after completing the first interview. Also, they have something to compare you to. This gives you the opportunity to set the bar and establish a high standard for others to have to match. During the time of the second interview the panelist or hiring authority are fresh and enthusiastic about finding the right person to lead the department. They are most attentive. As more candidates are being interviewed throughout the morning and afternoon, a combination of fatigue and/or disappointment can start to emerge. As the last person of the day, you now get to re-energize the panel or hiring authority and leave them with an indelible memory of your top performance.

---

There is a universal law regarding what it takes to be successful in life. Throughout the world many different cultures and religions have expressed it in a variety of ways, but they each have virtually the same meaning. Two such examples of this universal law are found in the Bible and in Buddhism. "As a man thinketh in his heart, so is he" and "All that we are is the result of what we have thought. The mind is everything. What we think, we become." To access this proven path to success, think about your goal at all times. I promise you, it shall come to fruition.

---

Never pursue a position unless you are truly willing to accept it. If you are unsure, then do the necessary research to determine if it is a good fit. Many use the excuse that they are applying for the experience of interviewing. If you set up practice interviews as suggested, you gain all the experience you need. You never want to be seen as someone who is simply looking for the next best opportunity, but is not willing to stay to make the changes needed. If panelists get the impression that you are simply applying for the experience, their concerns will eventually make its way to the scoring sheet.

---

Final thought and advice—In the pursuit of your ultimate goal, remember that true satisfaction and joy will not come unless you learn the importance of appreciation for each stage of the journey. This is to say that if you are only focused on getting to the ultimate goal and never appreciating your progress or each milestone along the way, when you do get to the top, it will have less meaning and could even be disappointing.

———————

Final, final thought and advice—There is a time for every season. This however is not the time to try and demonstrate how smart you may think you are. It is not the time to demonstrate how controlling you can be or how dominant you appear to be. It is the time to express your true views on key issues facing the community you would like to serve and various ways in which you can assist in addressing them. It is the time to express your values, and demonstrate credibility, and professionalism. It is the time to express how you will be value added.

———————

Final, final, final thought and advice—Once you have achieved your goal and have made a true difference in the delivery of quality service and enhanced public safety protection, please consider becoming a city manager or administrator. I have repeatedly shared with colleagues that fire and police chiefs are professionally trained and hard wired to manage a county, city or township. Why? Because they are accustomed to such important things as receiving streams of data and making difficult decisions in real time. When the decision outcome is not what was desired, you are not afraid to step back and reconsider other options. Timely decisions, adaptability and courage are three important traits of a great leader.

I look forward to reading about your ascension to the top!

Best

P. Lamont Ewell